TURN IT UP !

# Turn it up!

### 50 All-New, Fiery Recipes for Cooking with Chilies, Peppercorns, Mustard, Horseradish, and Ginger

by Janet Hazen

Photography by
Joyce Oudkerk Pool

CHRONICLE BOOKS

SAN FRANCISCO

Library of Congress Cataloging-in-Publication Data:

Hazen, Janet.
    Turn it up! : 50 all-new, fiery recipes for cooking with chilies,
peppercorns, mustard, horseradish, and ginger / by Janet Hazen ;
photography by Joyce Oudkerk Pool.
        p.    cm.
    Includes index.
    ISBN 0-8118-0633-2
    1. Cookery, International.   2. Condiments.   3 Spices.
I. Pool, Joyce Oudkerk.   II. Title.
TX725.A1H356   1995
641.59—dc20                                          94-13095
                                                        CIP

Edited by Carolyn Krebs
Book and cover design by Brenda Rae Eno
Food Styling by Robert Burns
Composition by Suzanne Scott
Printed in Hong Kong

Distributed in Canada by Raincoast Books,
8680 Cambie Street, Vancouver, B.C. V6P 6M9

10 9 8 7 6 5 4 3 2 1

Chronicle Books
275 Fifth Street
San Francisco, CA 94103

*For their contribution to this project, I wish to thank the many talented individuals at Chronicle Books; Carolyn Krebs for her fastidious copy editing, Joyce Oudkerk Pool for yet another magnificent collection of stunning photographs, and Robert Burns for his exquisite sense of style, and everyone for their never-ending wit and good humor.*

*I am most grateful to Leslie Jonath, Caroline Herter, and Bill LeBlond at Chronicle Books, and to my friends and colleagues for providing support during the final stages of this book.*

*Special thanks to life-long friend Jackie Holland, my family—Bruce Hazen, Jennifer Shirley, and Irene Hazen, to dear friends Julie Keating, Dorothy Londagin, Lorna Baird, and Sarah Byerly for their remarkable patience and listening abilities, and for lending comfort and assurance.*

# Contents

## Horseradish

*Pan-Fried Potato and Horseradish Cakes ~ 59*

*Green Bean Salad with Creamy Almond-Horseradish Dressing ~ 60*

*New Potato Salad with Sour Cream–Horseradish Dressing ~ 62*

*Smoked Ham and Cabbage Slaw with Horseradish ~ 63*

*Roast Beef and Vegetable Rolls with Horseradish Cream Cheese ~ 65*

*Smoked Chicken Salad with Horseradish Vinaigrette ~ 67*

*Pan-Fried Trout on Spinach with Bacon and Horseradish ~ 68*

*Rigatoni with Prawns and Horseradish-Leek Cream ~ 69*

*Israeli Horseradish and Beet Condiment ~ 70*

*Pork Tenderloin and Cucumber Sandwiches with Horseradish Mayonnaise ~ 73*

## Mustard

*Chinese-Style Mouth-Fire Dipping Sauce ~ 78*

*Creamy Mustard, Potato, and Leek Gratin ~ 79*

*Caramelized Onion-Mustard Tart with Gruyère Cheese ~ 81*

*Ham and Rice Salad with Two Mustards ~ 82*

*Melted Cheddar and Sweet Pickle Sandwiches with Two Mustards ~ 84*

*Sweet and Spicy Bell Pepper–Mustard Relish ~ 85*

*Mustard- and Honey-Braised Brussels Sprouts ~ 86*

*Baked Macaroni with Mustard and Cheddar Cheese ~ 89*

*Irene's Mustard-Glazed Ham Loaf ~ 90*

*Grilled Chicken Wings with Two Mustards and Honey ~ 92*

# $\mathcal{P}$EPPERCORNS

# *I*NTRODUCTION

CONSUMING SIZZLING-HOT, SPICY FOODS INDUCES TONGUE-SEARING, SINUS-CLEARING, throat-stinging, and chest-warming sensations that seduce and intoxicate. Once bitten by the fiery food bug, most devotees launch a never-ending search for ingredients guaranteed to generate that unmistakable high. They are enthralled with foods that flame the palate, bring tears to the eyes and sweat to the brow.

The scientific or, some might say, psychological explanation for this phenomenon is related to the human response to that well-known thin line between pain and pleasure. The theory is that once your mouth has been set ablaze, the brain releases endorphins, which produce a morphine-like reaction in the body (athletes, especially long-distance runners, also experience this reaction when exercising). Hence, the expression "It hurts so bad it feels good" holds true even in the gustatory realm.

The hot food craze has hit nearly every faction of our culinary world. Stories about torrid ingredients are featured on the front pages of newspaper food sections nationwide. Magazine articles on the subject appear on a regular basis, and there is at least one publication devoted solely to the topic of chili peppers. Restaurant diners are fearlessly experimenting with the incendiary dishes featured on Chinese, Thai, Vietnamese, Indian, and African menus. Home cooks now have the option of purchasing a wide range of fiery ingredients through mail-order catalogs and from stores that feature combustible comestibles from all over the world.

Fresh and dried chili peppers, the most popular source of culinary fire, still hold first place in terms of available firepower and their effect on the palate. Not to be overlooked, however, are such heat-lending ingredients as horseradish, mustard, peppercorns, and fresh ginger root.

Palate-awakening and blood-stimulating fresh horseradish root clears the head while providing a blast to the tongue. Until recently, this pungent condiment was primarily reserved as an accompaniment to roast beef and prime rib and for mixing with sour cream to serve with baked potatoes. Contemporary cooks, however, are finding broader culinary applications for the distinctively flavored root. More and more we see both fresh horseradish root and prepared horseradish paired with smoked and fresh fish, poultry, and meat dishes and in vegetable, grain, and potato salads.

Sparkling fresh, earthy, and pointed in flavor, fresh ginger root warms the mouth gently when cooked; raw it supplies a decided bite. Whether cooked or raw, pickled, candied, or preserved in brine, ginger has been a staple of most Asian kitchens for centuries. Dried and ground to a powder, American and European cooks have included powdered ginger in baked goods, in hot, spiced beverages, and even in ales and beer. In this book, the refreshing flavor of ginger adds a pleasant bite to a broad range of recipes.

Most people's familiarity with peppercorns is limited to the black pepper that sits atop the dining table in a miserable preground state, loaded with fillers and already stale when purchased. Black pepper is largely taken for granted, and most average kitchens do not contain white pepper, much less green or pink peppercorns. If you have yet to discover the virtues of cooking and seasoning with freshly ground peppercorns, whether black, white, green, or pink, then perhaps this book will serve as inspiration.

As of late, prepared mustards have taken the condiment spotlight, and it's about time. Regretably, many people have long ignored the exciting culinary potential of mustard. Until recently, the few conventional uses for mustard included smearing it on bread when making ham and cheese sandwiches, lining the top of a hot dog at baseball games, and occasionally adding it to cream sauces. Luckily, with so many delicious mustards on the market, the average consumer has moved away from these rather predictable and mundane uses and has embraced mustard as an indispensable condiment and cooking ingredient.

The recipes in this book are rated on a scale of 1 to 10, with 10 the hottest rating. There is a great deal of subjectivity in this area, however. Among five people, one food can provoke a different reaction in each. Generally speaking, we have similar tolerances for the temperature of food, but sensitivity to salty, sweet, pungent, and spicy qualities varies from one individual to the next. Therefore, the ratings applied to recipes in this collection may not correspond precisely to your particular palate. For this reason it's wise to view the ratings only as a general guideline.

Dedicated hotheads will find many delicious ways to walk the line between pleasure and pain within the chapters of this book, and the uninitiated may well become converts. A few dishes generate enough heat to earn the highest rating, others produce only a mild warming sensation, but all contain robustly flavored ingredients with distinctive character. Cook up some of these dishes and indulge in a meal saturated with invigorating flavors, fresh ingredients, healthful components, and seductive, fiery intensity.

# CHILIES

Chinese Chicken Salad with Spicy Peanut Sauce

Shrimp and Melon Salad with Cayenne-Serrano Vinaigrette

Ethiopian Onion- and Ginger-Stuffed Jalapeños

Chilled Tomato-Shrimp Bisque with Ancho
and Chipotle Chilies

Pants-on-Fire Black Bean Soup

Burmese Beef and Potato Coconut Curry

African Berbere Sauce

Zhoug—Israeli Chili Pepper Paste

Doro Wat—Ethiopian Chicken Stew

Chocolate-Coffee Brownies with Chipotle Chilies

# CHILIES

IN THE KINGDOM OF BLISTERING, SCORCHING-HOT FOODS, IT IS THE MIGHTY CHILI PEPPER THAT wears the crown. Whether yellow, orange, red, green, or deep violet in color, fresh and dried chili peppers—the fruit of species of the Capsicum genus—are universally popular in the world of incendiary foods.

Historical evidence suggests that chili peppers were a common cooking ingredient as early as 4000 B.C. The Aztecs and Mayans in Central and South America and Indians in the West Indies had used fresh chilies for centuries, but it wasn't until after Columbus's second journey to these regions in 1495 that chili peppers were introduced to the Old World. The Spanish returned home with the plant, where it thrived in the hot, sunny climate of the Mediterranean. Portuguese and Spanish traders spread the chili pepper on their travels to Africa, India, and the Far East, where they were quickly assimilated into the native cuisines. By the 1600s chili peppers had been introduced to virtually every region of the world.

Native to South America, chili peppers are now cultivated in India, Mexico, China, Indonesia, Thailand, and the United States—where New Mexico, Texas, California, Arizona, and Louisiana are the leading growers. Typically, chilies grow best in hot, humid climates with long growing seasons, but many varieties also do well in mild, temperate zones.

Flamboyant, assertive, and visually appealing, chili peppers can be mild and sweet, warm and complex, or painfully hot. It is difficult to differentiate and classify the hundreds of varieties; deviations within individual classes make it even harder to predict the level of heat contained within a given chili pepper. Since the capsaicin, contained primarily in the veins and seeds, is the element in chilies that dictates overall heat level, one way to determine the fire potential of a chili is by counting its veins and examining the quantity of seeds. Generally speaking, fruits with a higher ratio of veins and seeds to flesh are hotter than those with proportionately fewer veins and seeds. Additionally, those grown in hotter climates tend to be a bit more fiery. Even within the same variety there can be a range of intensities; a jalapeño grown in one area may differ greatly from another grown only two miles away.

In 1902, pharmacologist Wilber Scoville developed a method for measuring the amount, or power, of capsaicin in a given pepper. Originally, Scoville presented tasters with a mixture of ground chilies, sugar, alcohol, and water. Values were given according to the amount of diluting ingredients (sugar, alcohol, and water) necessary to make the mixture devoid of heat. Today computers perform this challenging task, rating peppers by Scoville Units, which indicate parts per million of capsaicin.

Next time you bite into a sizzling speck of edible fire and it happens to be a jalapeño chili pepper, remember this: The Scoville scale begins at zero with mild bell peppers, and moves into the lower mid-range, with the cascabel rating four (out of ten) and a unit measurement of 1,500 to 2,500. Relatively innocuous jalapeños rank dead center with a unit rating of 2,500 to 5,000. Cayenne, tabasco, aji, and piquin peppers, packed with approximately 30,000 to 50,000 Scoville Units, rank number eight out of ten. The scale tops off with the wicked and much-prized habanero and Bahamian chilies, which contain between 100,000 and 300,000 Scoville Units. In comparison, that minuscule little grain of jalapeño that seared your mouth is relatively benign.

With over four hundred varieties being grown today, the availability and assortment of fresh and dried chili peppers is staggering. If you cannot find the exact type of pepper called for in the following recipes, substitute one of similar size, color, and approximate heat intensity.

When purchasing fresh chili peppers, look for fruit that is firm, smooth, free of blemishes, and even colored. Store fresh chilies in a plastic bag in the refrigerator for up to two weeks. If your purchases begin to show signs of age and you have no immediate use for them, roast, peel, seed, and stem the chilies and either store in the freezer in a tightly sealed container for up to six to eight months, or cover with peanut or olive oil and store in a tightly sealed container in the refrigerator for up to two months. Alternatively, you can "pickle" the roasted peppers by covering them with a mild vinegar, or marinate them with a mixture of oil and vinegar and perhaps some garlic and herbs.

Dried peppers ought to be glossy and free of holes, tears, and insects (some prepackaged dried chili peppers imported from Mexico come with unexpected extras—tiny flying bugs).

Store dried chili peppers in tightly sealed plastic or paper bags in a cool, dark place for up to one year; six months is optimal. To rehydrate, place the chilies in a bowl and cover with hot or warm water (top with a smaller bowl filled with water to keep them submerged). Soak at room temperature until soft and pliable. Depending on the type of chili, this could take as little as fifteen minutes or as long as three hours. Generally speaking, the hotter the soaking liquid the faster the pepper rehydrates. However, some feel that boiling hot water brings out a bitter taste in dried chili peppers; I have yet to find this to be true.

Despite their reputation, not all dishes containing chili peppers are exceedingly torrid. Certainly not all of the recipes that follow will scorch your mouth, but a few potential palate-burners, such as *Ethiopian Onion-and Ginger-Stuffed Jalapeños* or *Chilled Tomato-Shrimp Bisque with Ancho and Chipotle Chilies,* could bring a tear to your eye.

Sensitive palates will appreciate the flavor-packed *Burmese Beef and Potato Coconut Curry* and the *Doro Wat* (Ethiopian chicken stew), two rich, satisfying dishes that improve with age up to three or four days. Both can easily be made twice as hot by doubling the amount of chili peppers. However, more is not necessarily better with all the recipes. Increasing the number of peppers called for in the *Shrimp and Melon Salad with Cayenne-Serrano Vinaigrette* or in the *Chocolate-Coffee Brownies with Chipotle Chilies* would destroy their delicate flavor balance by allowing one taste and one sensation to dominate. We all like to set our heads afire from time to time, but not every dish is designed to deliver a dose of capsaicin powerful enough to peel paint.

Two cautionary notes: When preparing fresh and dried chili peppers, either wear gloves or refrain from touching any mucus membranes until you're certain your hands are free from the natural oils. Even repeated hand washing with hot water and soap will not fully remove the capsaicin-containing oils. Secondly, if you happen to get in over your head during a typical hothead dining experience, and you suddenly find your mouth going into orbit, *do not drink water!* Consumption of water only intensifies the agonizing burning sensation. Instead, drink milk or eat some yogurt—even buttered bread, tortillas, or rice can help.

# Chinese Chicken Salad with Spicy Peanut Sauce

FRESH CHILI PEPPERS AND A GENEROUS DOSE OF PREPARED CHINESE HOT CHILI PASTE ADD FIRE AND SPARK TO THIS CLASSIC CHINESE CHICKEN SALAD. THE PEANUT SAUCE IS BEST IF PREPARED ONE TO TWO DAYS AHEAD.

**MAKES ABOUT 6 SERVINGS.** ~ **HOTTEST #9**

TO MAKE THE SPICY PEANUT SAUCE: In a medium bowl, combine the peanut butter, water, soy sauce, hoisin sauce, and vinegar, whisking with a wire whisk or fork to make a smooth emulsion. Add the sesame oil, garlic, ginger, serrano chilies, and chili paste; mix well. Season with salt and pepper, if desired. The sauce can be stored in a tightly sealed container in the refrigerator for up to 2 days. Bring to room temperature before serving.

Place the chicken breasts in a large pot and cover with cold water. Bring to a boil over high heat and cook 3 minutes. Remove from the heat and cover with a tight-fitting lid. Let stand at room temperature for at least 1 hour or up to 2 hours. Remove chicken from cooking liquid and cool to room temperature. When cool, remove the meat from the bones, taking care to separate the tendons and fat from the meat; discard all but the meat. Using your hands, shred the chicken into bite-size pieces.

Place the cabbage on a large platter and surround it with the cucumbers; top with the chicken. Spoon the sauce over the chicken and garnish with the cilantro and scallions. Serve at room temperature.

SPICY PEANUT SAUCE:

½ cup natural peanut butter

¼ cup water

4 tablespoons soy sauce

3 tablespoons hoisin sauce

2 tablespoons rice wine vinegar

1 tablespoon sesame oil

4 cloves garlic, minced

1½ tablespoons minced, peeled fresh ginger root

6 red serrano chili peppers, stemmed, seeded, and finely minced

2½ teaspoons Chinese hot chili paste

Salt and white pepper, to taste

3 large chicken breasts halves

4½ cups finely shredded white cabbage

½ English cucumber, peeled, halved lengthwise, and thinly sliced

¼ cup coarsely chopped fresh cilantro

⅓ cup finely chopped scallions

# Shrimp and Melon Salad with Cayenne-Serrano Vinaigrette

COOL, REFRESHING HONEYDEW MELON AND SUCCULENT PRAWNS FORM A SWEET-SAVORY BACKDROP FOR THIS SALAD'S SIZZLING-HOT VINAIGRETTE. THE COMBINATION OF RED AND GREEN HOT CHILI PEPPERS MAKES FOR A VERY STRIKING SALAD.

**MAKES 4 SERVINGS.** ~ **HOTTEST #7**

CAYENNE-SERRANO VINAIGRETTE:

½ cup peanut oil

2 tablespoons each fresh orange and lemon juice

1 teaspoon cayenne pepper

4 serrano chili peppers, stemmed, halved, seeded, and thinly sliced

Salt and pepper, to taste

SHRIMP AND MELON SALAD:

1 pound large prawns

1 small honeydew melon, cut into eighths, peeled, seeded, and cut into ⅛-inch-wide slices

⅓ cup finely chopped fresh mint leaves

TO MAKE THE CAYENNE-SERRANO VINAIGRETTE: Place the peanut oil in a small bowl. Slowly add the orange and lemon juices, whisking constantly with a wire whisk to form a smooth emulsion. Add the cayenne pepper and serrano chilies and mix well. Season with salt and pepper and set aside until needed.

Bring 3 quarts of water to boil in a 5-quart saucepan. Add the prawns and cook 1 to 1½ minutes, just until the prawns are opaque in the center. Take care not to overcook the prawns. Drain in a colander and refresh with cold water. Cool to room temperature. When cool enough to handle, remove the shells and tails and discard.

Arrange the melon and prawns on a large plate. Drizzle with the vinaigrette and garnish with the mint. Serve at cool room temperature.

# Ethiopian Onion- and Ginger-Stuffed Jalapeños

THIS IS MY RENDITION OF A TRADITIONAL DISH DESCRIBED TO ME BY AN ETHIOPIAN FRIEND.
NOT FOR THE FAINT OF HEART, IT IS MADE WITH FIERCE JALAPEÑO CHILIES STUFFED WITH A PIQUANT, FIERY,
GINGER-ACCENTED FILLING. THIS IS THE QUINTESSENTIAL APPETIZER FOR HOTHEADS.

**MAKES 8 TO 12 SERVINGS. ∾ HOTTEST #10**

In a 3-quart saucepan, bring 2 quarts of salted water to boil over high heat. Add the jalapeño peppers and cook 1 minute. Drain in a colander, refresh with cold water, and immediately transfer to a bowl filled with ice water. When the chili peppers are thoroughly chilled, drain in a colander and pat dry with a clean kitchen towel.

Using a sharp paring knife, on each chili make a ½-inch-long incision across the pepper, just under the stem. Starting at the right side of the incision, cut lengthwise along the pepper, making one side of a V-shaped cut, stopping approximately ¼ inch before the tip. Return to the left side of the cross-wise incision, make another V-shaped cut down to the bottom of the chili pepper, and remove the triangular piece of flesh. You should have a narrow, V-shaped opening. Carefully remove and discard the seeds, taking care not to tear the peppers. Set aside until needed.

In a large sauté pan, cook the onion and cumin in the butter over moderately high heat for 5 minutes, stirring frequently. Add the garlic and ginger and cook 2 to 3 minutes, stirring frequently. Season with salt and pepper and cool to room temperature. Dividing equally, gently stuff each jalapeño with the filling, taking care not to tear the flesh. Garnish with the serrano chilies and serve at room temperature.

*12 large jalapeño chili peppers*

*1 medium onion, minced*

*1 teaspoon ground cumin*

*2 tablespoons unsalted butter*

*4 cloves garlic, minced*

*4-inch piece fresh ginger root, peeled and minced*

*Salt and pepper, to taste*

*3 red serrano chili peppers (or any other red chili pepper), stemmed, seeded, and minced, for garnish*

# Chilled Tomato-Shrimp Bisque with Ancho and Chipotle Chilies

I PREFER THE CONTRASTING EFFECT OF SPICY, PIQUANT FLAVORS COMBINED WITH A COLD SERVING TEMPERATURE IN
THIS SIMPLE-TO-PREPARE SOUP, BUT IF YOU'RE PRESSED FOR TIME, FEEL FREE TO SERVE IT IMMEDIATELY, PIPING HOT.
PAIR WITH A GREEN SALAD AND WARM BREAD FOR A COMPLETE MEAL.
**MAKES ABOUT 6 SERVINGS. ∼ HOTTEST #9**

*1 large red onion, coarsely chopped*

*3 cloves garlic, coarsely chopped*

*4 red jalapeño chili peppers, stemmed, seeded,
and coarsely chopped*

*¼ cup olive oil*

*4 dried ancho chili peppers, stemmed and
coarsely chopped*

*4 dried chipotle chili peppers, stemmed and
coarsely chopped, or 2 tablespoons canned
chipotle chili peppers in adobo sauce, chopped*

*6 large tomatoes, cored and coarsely chopped*

*2 cups water*

*5 cups light chicken stock*

*1 cup heavy cream*

*Salt and pepper, to taste*

*1 pound small shrimp, peeled and
coarsely chopped*

*½ cup finely chopped fresh parsley*

In a very large, heavy-bottomed pot, cook the onion, garlic, and jalapeño peppers in the olive oil over moderate heat for 5 minutes, stirring frequently. Add the ancho and chipotle chilies and tomatoes and cook 5 minutes, stirring frequently. Add the water and chicken stock and bring to a boil over high heat; cook 5 minutes, stirring frequently. Reduce the heat to moderate and simmer 30 minutes, stirring occasionally. Remove from the heat and cool to room temperature.

In a blender, puree the mixture in batches until smooth. Strain through a fine wire sieve and return to the saucepan. Add the cream and bring to a boil over high heat, stirring constantly to prevent the mixture from boiling over. Reduce the heat to moderate and cook 15 to 20 minutes, stirring often, or until the mixture is the consistency of heavy cream. Season with salt and pepper. Add the shrimp, mix well, and remove from the heat. To serve cold, cool to room temperature and refrigerate in a tightly sealed container for at least 6 hours, or up to 3 days. Serve garnished with the parsley.

# Pants-on-Fire Black Bean Soup

IF YOU PREFER A COMPLETELY VEGETARIAN VERSION OF THIS MOUTH-SEARING SOUP, SUBSTITUTE
VEGETABLE STOCK OR WATER FOR THE CHICKEN STOCK. CONVERSELY, FOR A MEATIER, MORE SUBSTANTIAL DISH,
ADD DICED SMOKED HAM OR COOKED AND CHOPPED BACON DURING THE LAST TWENTY MINUTES OF COOKING.
**MAKES ABOUT 8 SERVINGS.** ⁓ **HOTTEST #10**

Soak the beans in 8 cups of cold water overnight, changing the water once or twice. Drain the beans and place in a large, heavy-bottomed saucepan with the cascabel, de árbol, ancho, and pasilla chilies and 5 quarts of fresh water. Bring to a boil over high heat. Reduce the heat to moderate and simmer for 1 hour and 40 minutes, or until the beans are tender.

Meanwhile, in a very large, heavy-bottomed sauté pan, cook the onions, garlic, jalapeño peppers, spices, red pepper flakes, and herbs in the olive oil over moderate heat for 5 minutes, stirring constantly. Add the tomatoes and chipotle chilies and cook 5 minutes, stirring frequently. Add to the black beans along with the chicken stock; bring to a boil over high heat. Reduce the heat to moderate and simmer for 30 to 40 minutes, stirring from time to time.

Remove 6 cups of the soup and puree in batches in a blender until fairly smooth. Return to the pot and mix well. Add the lime juice and season with salt and pepper. Just before serving, garnish with the cilantro.

*2 cups dried black beans, washed and sorted*

*6 cascabel chili peppers, stemmed, seeded, and finely chopped*

*5 de árbol or cayenne chili peppers, stemmed*

*3 ancho chili peppers, stemmed, seeded, and finely chopped*

*1 pasilla chili pepper, stemmed, seeded, and finely chopped*

*2 medium onions, cut into small dice*

*4 cloves garlic, finely chopped*

*4 jalapeño chili peppers, stemmed, seeded, and coarsely chopped*

*1 tablespoon each ground cumin and coriander*

*2½ teaspoons dried red pepper flakes*

*1½ teaspoons each dried oregano and sage*

*3 tablespoons olive or vegetable oil*

*2 tomatoes, cored and finely chopped*

*2 tablespoons canned chipotle chili peppers in adobo sauce, minced*

*6 cups chicken stock*

*½ cup fresh lime juice*

*Salt and pepper, to taste*

*1 cup coarsely chopped fresh cilantro*

# Burmese Beef and Potato Coconut Curry

Tender beef chunks and potatoes accented with aromatic spices, assorted hot chili peppers, and sweet coconut milk meld together in this rich and satisfying stew. Serve with steamed rice and stir-fried green beans.

**Makes 6 servings.** ∽ **Hottest #9**

5 tablespoons peanut oil

2 pounds beef stew meat, cut into 1-inch cubes

2 medium onions, cut into large dice

4 cloves garlic, finely chopped

8 serrano chili peppers, stemmed and thinly sliced

5 jalapeño chili peppers, stemmed, seeded, and thinly sliced

1 tablespoon each ground cumin and coriander

2 teaspoons each ground fennel seeds and turmeric

1½ teaspoons cayenne pepper

Two 13½-ounce cans unsweetened coconut milk

1 cup water

3 medium boiling potatoes (about 1 pound), peeled and cut into ½-inch cubes

½ cup fresh lime juice

Salt and pepper, to taste

3 red serrano chili peppers (or any other small red chili pepper), stemmed and thinly sliced

½ cup finely chopped fresh cilantro, for garnish

In a very large nonstick sauté pan, heat 2 tablespoons of the oil over high heat. Add the beef and cook, stirring frequently, until golden brown on all sides. Remove with a slotted spoon and set aside.

In the same pan, add the remaining 3 tablespoons oil and heat until hot but not smoking. Add the onions, garlic, chili peppers, and spices and cook 7 to 8 minutes, stirring frequently. Transfer to a large, heavy-bottomed pot and add the beef. Cook the mixture over high heat for 3 minutes, stirring constantly.

Add the coconut milk and water and bring to a boil. Reduce the heat to moderate and cook 1 hour and 15 minutes, or until the meat is very tender. Add the potatoes and lime juice and cook 10 to 12 minutes, or until the potatoes are tender when pierced with a fork. Season with salt and pepper. Just before serving, garnish with the serrano chilies and cilantro.

# African Berbere Sauce

Berbere, THE OFFICIAL LANGUAGE OF ETHIOPIA, IS ALSO THE NAME GIVEN TO THIS INCENDIARY RED PEPPER SAUCE. USED BOTH AS A TABLE CONDIMENT AND AS AN INGREDIENT IN MANY SOUPS, STEWS, MARINADES, AND MEAT DISHES, Berbere PLAYS A VERY IMPORTANT ROLE IN THE COOKING OF ETHIOPIA, AND CAN BE A VALUABLE INGREDIENT FOR AMERICAN COOKS, AS WELL.

*When you prepare this intoxicating, brick-red chili sauce, be sure to use your overhead stove fan or open all the windows. You might also want to tie a scarf around your nose and mouth while heating the spices in the sauté pan.*

**MAKES ABOUT 2 CUPS.** ⌒ **HOTTEST #9**

Place the red pepper flakes, cumin, black pepper, salt, cardamom, fenugreek, nutmeg, cloves, cinnamon, allspice, and coriander in a medium, heavy-bottomed nonstick sauté pan. Cook over moderate heat, stirring constantly, until their aroma fills the air and the color has darkened slightly, about 4 minutes. Transfer to a blender and set aside.

In the same pan, heat the cayenne pepper and paprika over moderately low heat for 4 to 5 minutes, stirring constantly. Add to the spice mixture in the blender along with the garlic, water, and peanut oil. Puree until smooth, stopping occasionally to scrape the sides of the container.

Return the pureed mixture to the sauté pan and cook over moderately low heat for 10 to 12 minutes, stirring frequently to prevent the sauce from burning. Remove from the heat and cool to room temperature. Store in a tightly sealed container in the refrigerator for up to 5 months.

*3 to 5 tablespoons dried red pepper flakes*

*2 teaspoons each ground cumin, black pepper, and kosher or sea salt*

*½ teaspoon each ground cardamom, fenugreek, nutmeg, cloves, cinnamon, allspice, and coriander*

*1¼ cups cayenne pepper*

*3 tablespoons paprika*

*6 cloves garlic, minced*

*2 cups water*

*3 tablespoons peanut oil*

# ZHOUG—*Israeli Chili Pepper Paste*

SIZZLING HOT AND FRAGRANT WITH FRESH HERBS, THIS SNAPPY JALAPEÑO PASTE
CAN BE USED WITH GRILLED MEATS, FISH, AND POULTRY; AS A BOOSTER FOR SOUPS AND STEWS;
OR MIXED WITH FRESH, FINELY CHOPPED TOMATOES, AS THEY DO IN THE MIDDLE EAST.
**MAKES ABOUT 1 CUP. ∽ HOTTEST #7**

*12 green jalapeño chili peppers, stemmed and seeded*

*3 cloves garlic*

*¾ cup loosely packed fresh parsley leaves*

*½ cup loosely packed fresh cilantro leaves*

*1½ tablespoons water*

*1½ teaspoons each ground cumin and cayenne pepper*

*1 teaspoon each kosher salt and pepper*

Place the jalapeño peppers and garlic in the bowl of a food processor. Process until smooth. Add the parsley, cilantro, water, spices, salt, and pepper. Process until smooth. Transfer to a nonreactive container, cover tightly, and store in the refrigerator for up to 3 months.

# DORO WAT—*Ethiopian Chicken Stew*

RECIPES CONTAINING THE WORD *WAT* ARE CONSIDERED NATIONAL DISHES OF ETHIOPIA. *INJERA*, THE SPONGY, BLAND,
PLIABLE FLAT BREAD TRADITIONALLY SERVED WITH THIS FIERY EAST AFRICAN STEW CAN BE PURCHASED READY-MADE
AT A LOCAL AFRICAN RESTAURANT, OR PREPARED FROM SCRATCH. ALTERNATELY, SERVE ITALIAN BREAD WITH THIS
FLAMING HOT STEW, AND RICE OR CRACKED WHEAT AS A COMPANION.

**MAKES ABOUT 4 SERVINGS.** ⁓ **HOTTEST #10**

4 tablespoons unsalted butter

2 large onions, halved and cut into
½-inch-wide slices

6 cloves garlic, finely chopped

2 teaspoons cayenne pepper

1 teaspoon each ground cardamom, cumin,
fennel seeds, and nutmeg

½ cup African *Berbere Sauce (see page 29)*

¼ cup tomato paste

4 chicken thighs

4 chicken legs

2½ cups chicken stock

4 hard-cooked eggs, pierced all over ¼-inch deep
with a fork and halved

Salt and pepper, to taste

½ cup finely chopped fresh cilantro

In a very large, heavy-bottomed saucepan, melt the butter over moderate heat. Add the onions, garlic, cayenne pepper, and spices and cook 15 minutes, stirring frequently. Add the *Berbere* sauce, tomato paste, and chicken and cook 10 minutes, stirring frequently. Add the stock and bring to a boil over high heat. Reduce the heat to moderate and simmer 1 hour, or until the chicken is very tender. Add the eggs and cook 10 minutes. Season with salt and pepper. Just before serving, garnish with the cilantro.

NOTE: To make hard-cooked eggs, place room-temperature eggs in a saucepan and generously cover with cold water. Bring to a boil over high heat and cook 1½ minutes. Remove from the heat and cover tightly. Let stand at room temperature for 1 hour. Remove the eggs, rap gently on a hard surface, and peel.

# Chocolate-Coffee Brownies with Chipotle Chilies

CHOCOLATE LOVERS WILL EXPERIENCE A REAL SURPRISE WHEN THEY BITE INTO THESE DENSE, RICH BROWNIES.
HOTHEADS WILL DELIGHT!

**MAKES ABOUT 6 SERVINGS.** ◦ **HOTTER #6**

Soak the chilies in hot water for 30 minutes, or until they are soft. Drain well and set aside.

Preheat oven to 350°F. Grease and lightly flour an 8-by-8-inch baking pan.

In a small saucepan, melt the butter and 5 ounces of the chocolate over low heat, stirring frequently. Add the ground coffee and reserved chilies and mix well. Cool to room temperature.

Place the sugar and eggs in a large bowl. Using a large kitchen spoon, beat until light in color and smooth, about 2 minutes. Add the chocolate mixture. Add the flour, salt, walnuts, and remaining 3 ounces of chocolate; mix until just combined. Pour the batter into the prepared pan and smooth the surface with a dull knife.

Bake on the lower shelf of the oven for 20 minutes. Rotate to the upper shelf and bake 30 minutes, or until the center is just set. Remove from the oven and cool to room temperature. When cool, run a dull knife around the edge of the pan and cut the brownies into squares. Serve immediately or wrap tightly in plastic wrap or aluminum foil and store at room temperature for up to 3 days.

*3 to 4 dried chipotle chili peppers, stemmed, seeded, and finely chopped*

*3 dried pepperoncini or any other tiny dried chili peppers, stemmed, seeded, and finely chopped*

*6 ounces unsalted butter (1½ sticks)*

*8 ounces semisweet chocolate, coarsely chopped*

*1½ tablespoons finely ground dark-roast coffee beans*

*1½ cups sugar*

*3 eggs, lightly beaten*

*1 cup all-purpose flour*

*Pinch salt*

*¾ cup coarsely chopped walnuts*

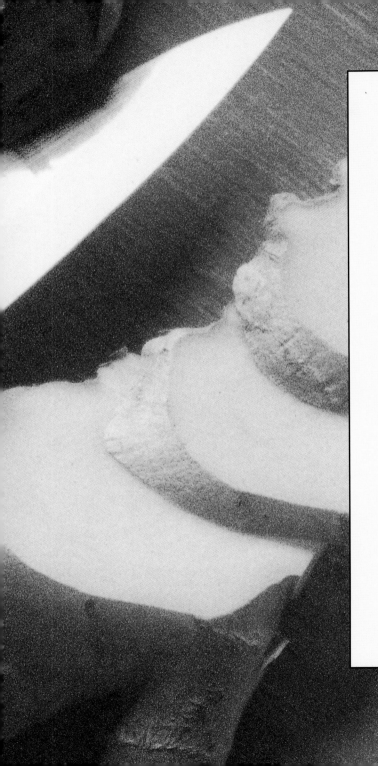

# GINGER

*Gingered Chicken Liver Spread with Currants*

*Ginger Chicken Salad with Cashew Nuts*

*Burmese Prawn Salad with Fried Shallots and Ginger*

*Chinese Stir-Fried Beef with Ginger*

*Cold Noodles with Asian Vegetables
and Ginger Peanut Sauce*

*Gingered Spring Vegetable and Salmon Soup*

*Apricot-Ginger Chutney*

*Pickled Ginger*

*Spiced Ginger Cake with Candied Ginger Cream*

*Apple, Ginger, and Mint Sorbet*

# $\mathcal{G}$INGER

UNTIL FAIRLY RECENTLY, MANY AMERICANS CONSIDERED FRESH GINGER AN EXOTIC INGREDIENT. Now, however, cooks are borrowing from the many cultures that have traditionally used the flavorful root in their cookery. Highly treasured by Asian and Indian cooks, both fresh and powdered ginger also frequently appear in the cuisines of Africa and the Caribbean. Although in this country ginger has generally been reserved for preparing these ethnic cuisines, inventive American chefs have broadened the use of fresh ginger root by incorporating it into other cuisines and by pairing it with new and unexpected ingredients.

Ginger plants grow best when planted in rich sandy soil in hot, humid, rainy climates. Hawaii, Fiji, the Caribbean, Costa Rica, Guatemala, Nicaragua, Australia, India, and China are the primary growers of fresh ginger. China and India are the biggest producers and exporters of powdered ginger, a form used primarily for baked goods and in beverages. Crystallized ginger is usually eaten as a candy or as an after-dinner palate refresher, but it is also used for decorating and garnishing baked goods and other confections. Vinegared ginger is a mainstay of Japanese cuisine that is most often paired with sushi or sashimi.

Fresh ginger root is versatile and easy to use in both sweet and savory dishes. Depending on how it is used, the flavor of ginger can range from bitingly sharp and spicy to mild and gently warm. As a result, it is compatible with a wide assortment of foods. Reflecting the multifaceted quality of this rhizome, the recipes in this chapter are not limited to Asian or Indian fare, nor are all recipes exceedingly fiery.

Warmed, rather than set afire by fresh ginger, are such dishes as *Gingered Spring Vegetable and Salmon Soup, Cold Noodles and Asian Vegetables with Ginger Peanut Sauce,* and the moist and delicious *Spiced Ginger Cake with Candied Ginger Cream.* Hotter and more piquant are such traditional dishes as *Chinese Stir-Fried Beef with Ginger* and *Apricot-Ginger Chutney.* The icy-hot *Apple, Ginger, and Mint Sorbet* also packs quite a punch!

When purchasing fresh ginger, look for very hard roots with smooth, unblemished, light brown skin; the "hand," as the root is often referred to, should not yield to finger pressure and ought to be free of cuts or dents. Like other fresh produce, it's best to use ginger as soon as possible, but if you need to store it, wrap it tightly in plastic wrap and store in the vegetable bin of your refrigerator. When stored in this manner, fresh ginger will retain its flavor and texture for up to two weeks. It can be stored longer with some success, but rhizomes way past their prime are dry and flavorless.

When eating or cooking with fresh ginger, always remove the outer skin; exceptions to this principle include recipes in which ginger is used for flavoring only and removed at the end of cooking. Young ginger, which is less common in markets, does not require peeling since the skin is very thin and mild tasting and therefore edible.

To PEEL GINGER: Using a sharp paring knife, carefully remove the tough, outer layer of light brown skin and discard. If you are using the entire "hand," first remove the nubs or branches to facilitate peeling.

To CUT GINGER INTO SLIVERS: Peel the root and cut at an angle to produce oval shapes about ⅛ inch thick. Lay the flat oval shapes on the cutting board so that they barely overlap. Cutting the long way on the oval, slice into very thin, long pieces.

To FINELY CHOP GINGER: Peel the root, cut lengthwise into thin strips, and continue chopping until the ginger pieces are uniformly smaller than ⅛ inch.

To MINCE GINGER: Peel the root, cut lengthwise into thin strips, and continue chopping until the ginger is cut into minuscule pieces.

To DICE GINGER: Peel the root and slice one very thin piece from one side. Lay the root on the cutting board on the flat, cut side. Slice the root lengthwise; ⅛ inch wide for very small dice, ¼ inch wide for medium dice, and ½ inch wide for large dice. Stack the slices of ginger and cut again lengthwise into the desired-size strips. Make the final cuts by slicing across into the appropriate-size dice.

To GRATE GINGER: Peel the root and grate on a metal grater. Use the finest setting if you want mostly juice, medium for some pulp and a little juice, and the jumbo or coarsest setting for small bits of the root.

The circumference of ginger roots can be as thick as a silver dollar and as narrow as a nickel, but most roots are about the thickness of a quarter. The recipes following specify amounts in length measurements, and since this isn't exact, following are yields in standard cup measures for varying lengths of an average-size ginger root when finely chopped. You really don't have to use exact measurements of ginger, but some cooks feel better with more specific guidelines.

2-INCH PIECE GINGER ROOT = ABOUT 3 TABLESPOONS, FINELY CHOPPED

4-INCH PIECE GINGER ROOT = ABOUT ½ CUP, FINELY CHOPPED

6-INCH PIECE GINGER ROOT = ABOUT ⅔ CUP, FINELY CHOPPED

8-INCH PIECE GINGER ROOT = ABOUT 1 CUP, FINELY CHOPPED

# Gingered Chicken Liver Spread with Currants

BRIGHT-TASTING FRESH GINGER PROVIDES AN EXCELLENT COUNTERBALANCE TO THE RICH FLAVOR AND DENSE TEXTURE OF CHICKEN LIVERS. SERVE THIS SPREAD WITH CRACKERS, CROUTONS, OR TOASTED BREAD AND A SMALL BOWL OF CORNICHONS.

**MAKES 6 TO 8 SERVINGS.** ∼ **HOT #1**

In a small bowl, soak the currants in the sherry for 30 minutes at room temperature. Drain the currants, reserving the sherry. Set both aside until needed.

In a large sauté pan, cook the onion and garlic in the olive oil over moderate heat for 5 minutes, stirring frequently. Add the reserved sherry and cook until the liquid has evaporated, 3 to 4 minutes. Add the chicken livers and coriander and cook 5 to 6 minutes, or until the livers are tender and barely pink in the center. Add the ginger and soy sauce and mix well. Remove from the heat and cool slightly.

Place the mixture in a food processor. Pulsing on and off, process the mixture until smooth. If you do not have a food processor, place the mixture on a flat cutting board, and, using a large knife or cleaver, finely mince until the mixture is smooth.

Transfer to a bowl and add the reserved currants; mix well. Season with salt and pepper. Place a piece of plastic wrap directly on the surface of the spread, cover tightly, and refrigerate for at least 4 hours or up to 4 days.

*½ cup currants*

*¾ cup dry sherry*

*1 medium onion, coarsely chopped*

*2 cloves garlic, coarsely chopped*

*3 tablespoons olive oil*

*1 pound chicken livers, coarsely chopped*

*2 teaspoons ground coriander*

*3-inch piece fresh ginger root, peeled and minced*

*1 tablespoon soy sauce*

*Salt and pepper, to taste*

# Ginger Chicken Salad with Cashew Nuts

GINGER AND MAYONNAISE ARE A SELDOM-SEEN DUO, BUT I FIND THAT THE SHARP, PUNGENT, SLIGHTLY SWEET TASTE OF FRESH GINGER ROOT PLEASINGLY OFFSETS THE RICH QUALITY OF MAYONNAISE AND CASHEW NUTS IN THIS DISTINCTIVE SALAD.

**MAKES 4 TO 6 SERVINGS.** ∽ **HOT #1**

4 chicken breast halves

6-inch piece fresh ginger root, coarsely chopped

1 large bunch scallions, trimmed and finely chopped

1 cup water chestnuts, halved

5-inch piece fresh ginger root, peeled and
  finely chopped

1¼ cups mayonnaise (preferably homemade)

¼ cup fresh lemon juice

Salt and pepper, to taste

1 cup roasted cashews

Watercress, for lining platter

In a 6-quart pot, place the chicken breasts, 4 quarts of cold water, and the coarsely chopped ginger. Bring to a boil over high heat. Using a slotted spoon, remove the foam from the surface and discard. Reduce the heat to moderately low and cook approximately 15 minutes, until the chicken is opaque in the center. Take care not to overcook the chicken. Drain in a colander and cool the chicken to room temperature.

When cool enough to handle, keeping the breast meat intact, remove the skin, bones, tendons, cartilage, and fat; discard. Cut the chicken into ½-inch chunks and place in a large bowl along with the scallions, water chestnuts, finely chopped ginger, mayonnaise, and lemon juice. Mix gently and season with salt and pepper. Serve immediately or store in a tightly sealed container in the refrigerator for up to 3 days. Just before serving, add the cashews and mix well. Serve on a platter covered with watercress.

# Burmese Prawn Salad with Fried Shallots and Ginger

CHARACTERISTIC OF MANY SOUTHEAST ASIAN DISHES, THIS PALATE-AWAKENING SALAD DEPENDS ON A VARIETY
OF CONTRASTING INGREDIENTS FOR ITS STIMULATING TEXTURE AND FLAVOR.

**MAKES 6 SERVINGS.** ∽ **HOT #2**

¾ pound small prawns

5 tablespoons peanut oil

4 large shallots, halved and thinly sliced

4-inch piece fresh ginger root, peeled and
   finely chopped

2 tablespoons light soy sauce

2 tablespoons fresh lime juice

1 tablespoon fish sauce (Nuoc Cham)

3-inch piece fresh ginger root, peeled and minced

2 cloves garlic, minced

2½ cups finely shredded white cabbage

1 medium onion, halved and thinly sliced

⅓ cup finely chopped fresh cilantro, for garnish

Bring 2 quarts of water to boil in a large saucepan. Add the prawns, stir well, and cook 1 minute. Immediately drain in a colander and refresh with cold water. Transfer to a bowl filled with cold water and let stand 5 minutes. Drain well. Peel the prawns and remove tails; set aside until needed.

In a medium sauté pan, heat 3 tablespoons of the peanut oil over moderately high heat. When the oil is hot but not smoking, add the shallots and cook 4 minutes, stirring constantly, until they are golden brown and crisp. Add the finely chopped ginger and cook 2 or 3 minutes. Remove from the pan and drain on paper towels. Set aside until needed.

In a large bowl, combine the remaining 2 tablespoons peanut oil with the soy sauce, whisking constantly with a wire whisk to form a smooth emulsion. Add the lime juice, fish sauce, minced ginger and garlic; mix well. Add the cabbage, onion, and half of the prawns; toss gently. Arrange on a large platter, top with the remaining prawns, and garnish with the fried shallot-ginger mixture and the cilantro. Serve immediately.

# Chinese Stir-Fried Beef with Ginger

To facilitate slicing the beef, wrap it in plastic and place in the freezer for thirty minutes prior to cutting. This classic Chinese dish is best served with a large bowl of steamed rice or with cooked Chinese noodles.

**Makes about 4 servings.** ⁓Hot #3

In a nonreactive bowl, combine the beef, soy sauce, sherry, vinegar, white pepper, sugar, and garlic; mix well and let stand at room temperature for 30 to 40 minutes. Using your fingers, lift the meat from the bowl and gently squeeze the excess liquid from the meat back into the bowl. Add the cornstarch, oyster sauce, and chicken broth to the liquid and mix well; set aside.

In a very large, nonstick sauté pan or wok, heat the oil over high heat until it just begins to smoke. Immediately add the meat and ginger and cook 30 seconds, stirring constantly. Add the cornstarch mixture and the scallions and cook 1½ minutes, stirring constantly, until the sauce is thick and aromatic. Remove from the pan and serve immediately, garnished with the sesame seeds.

*1 pound beef flank steak, cut across the grain into slices about 1½ inches long and ⅛ inch thick*

*¼ cup soy sauce*

*¼ cup dry sherry*

*¼ cup rice wine vinegar*

*2 teaspoons white pepper*

*1 teaspoon sugar*

*3 cloves garlic, finely chopped*

*2 teaspoons cornstarch*

*1½ tablespoons oyster sauce*

*⅔ cup low-sodium chicken broth or water*

*2 tablespoons peanut oil*

*4½-inch piece fresh ginger root, peeled and slivered*

*6 scallions, trimmed and sliced into 1-inch pieces*

*1½ tablespoons sesame seeds, for garnish*

# Cold Noodles with Asian Vegetables and Ginger Peanut Sauce

PRESENTED AS A LIGHT SUPPER OR A COMPLETE LUNCH, THIS COLORFUL AND HEALTHFUL ROOM-TEMPERATURE
SALAD IS TERRIFIC DURING THE WARM-WEATHER MONTHS.

**MAKES 4 TO 6 SERVINGS.** ~HOT #3

Bring 3 quarts of salted water to boil in a 6-quart pot. Add the noodles and cook 6 to 7 minutes, or until they are al dente. Drain in a colander and refresh with cold water. Spread the noodles on kitchen towels or on layers of paper towels and pat dry. Transfer to a large bowl and add the bell pepper, snow peas, scallions, and cilantro. Set aside.

TO MAKE THE GINGER PEANUT SAUCE: In a medium bowl, combine the peanut and sesame oils. Slowly add the lime juice, whisking constantly with a wire whisk to form a smooth emulsion. Slowly add the soy sauce, whisking constantly. Add the ginger, garlic, and chilies and mix well. Season with salt and pepper.

Add three fourths of the ginger peanut sauce and three fourths of the peanuts to the noodle-vegetable mixture; toss gently. Mound the salad in the center of a large platter. Arrange the cucumbers around the edge of the salad. Drizzle with the remaining sauce and garnish with the remaining peanuts. Serve immediately.

¾ pound round Chinese egg noodles
   (preferably fresh)

1 small red bell pepper, stemmed, seeded, and slivered

¼ pound snow peas, blanched, trimmed,
   and thinly sliced lengthwise

4 scallions, trimmed and finely chopped

½ cup finely chopped fresh cilantro

GINGER PEANUT SAUCE:

1 cup peanut oil

1 tablespoon sesame oil

3 tablespoons fresh lime juice

2 tablespoons light soy sauce

4-inch piece fresh ginger root, peeled and minced

3 cloves garlic, minced

2 serrano chili peppers, stemmed and thinly sliced

Salt and pepper, to taste

¾ cup finely chopped roasted peanuts

½ English cucumber, thinly sliced

# Gingered Spring Vegetable and Salmon Soup

ACCENTED WITH FRESH GINGER, THE BRILLIANT COLORS AND WELCOMING FLAVOR OF
SPRING VEGETABLES FORM THE PERFECT BACKDROP FOR TENDER NEW POTATOES AND SUCCULENT
CHUNKS OF FRESH SALMON IN THIS MEMORABLE SOUP.

**MAKES ABOUT 6 SERVINGS.** ～ **HOT #1**

*1 teaspoon saffron threads*

*½ cup dry white wine*

*6 cups clam juice*

*2 shallots, halved and thinly sliced*

*6-inch piece fresh ginger root, peeled and slivered*

*6 tiny red new potatoes, quartered*

*1 pound boneless salmon filet, cut into
1-inch cubes*

*1 small red bell pepper, stemmed, seeded, and
cut into tiny triangles or squares*

*6 spears asparagus, trimmed and sliced on the
diagonal into ½-inch-long pieces*

*1 large ear white corn, shaved (about 1 cup
corn kernels)*

*4 tablespoons unsalted butter, cut into 8 pieces
(optional)*

*Salt and pepper, to taste*

In a small bowl, dissolve the saffron in the wine by rubbing the threads together until the liquid is orange and aromatic.

In a 4-quart saucepan, place the saffron-wine mixture, clam juice, shallots, and ginger. Bring to a boil over high heat and cook 5 minutes, stirring occasionally. Add the potatoes, reduce the heat to moderately high, and cook 15 or 20 minutes, or until they are tender when pierced with a fork. Add the salmon and cook 2 minutes. Add the red bell pepper, asparagus, corn, and butter (if desired) and cook 1½ minutes, or until the salmon is just cooked. Take care not to overcook the salmon. Season with salt and pepper and serve immediately.

# Apricot-Ginger Chutney

AT ONCE TART, SWEET, AND SPICY, THIS CHUTNEY IS AN EXCELLENT COMPANION TO POULTRY OR PORK,
OR TO SHARP CHEDDAR CHEESE AND CRACKERS.
**MAKES ABOUT 2¼ CUPS.** ∽ **HOT #3**

1 medium red onion, cut into small dice

2 cloves garlic, finely chopped

2 tablespoons peanut oil

½ teaspoon each ground cardamom, coriander,
   fennel seeds, anise, and fenugreek

½ cup water

5-inch piece fresh ginger root, peeled and
   finely chopped

6 large apricots, pitted and coarsely chopped

⅓ cup fresh lemon juice

Salt and pepper, to taste

In a large, shallow saucepan, cook the onion and garlic in the peanut oil over moderate heat for 5 minutes, stirring frequently. Add the spices and cook 2 minutes, stirring constantly. Add the water and cook 5 to 7 minutes, or until it has evaporated. Add the ginger, apricots, and lemon juice and cook 15 to 20 minutes, stirring occasionally, until the mixture is thick and aromatic. Season with salt and pepper. Store in a tightly sealed container in the refrigerator for up to 10 days.

# Pickled Ginger

FOR A TRADITIONAL PRESENTATION, PAIR THIS INVIGORATING CONDIMENT WITH SUSHI OR SASHIMI.
FOR LESS CONVENTIONAL APPLICATIONS, BRIGHTEN THE FLAVOR OF SAUTÉED POULTRY, FISH, SEAFOOD, OR MEAT DISHES,
OR VEGETABLE, PASTA OR RICE SALADS BY ADDING THE PICKLED SLICES WHOLE OR FINELY CHOPPED.
**MAKES 2 CUPS.** ∽ **HOT #6**

*When making pickled ginger, look for young ginger in Asian grocery stores and produce markets.*
*If you cannot locate this tender, juicy variety, use regular ginger and peel before slicing.*

Arrange the sliced ginger in a single layer in a large, nonreactive baking pan. Sprinkle with the salt and cover with plastic wrap. Let sit overnight at room temperature. Transfer to a glass container large enough to accommodate the remaining ingredients. Add the vinegar and sugar; cover tightly and shake vigorously to combine the ingredients. Refrigerate for at least 1 week before serving. The ginger will keep for up to 3 months if stored in the refrigerator. Drain slightly before serving.

*1 pound fresh young ginger root, sliced crosswise into paper-thin rounds*

*1½ tablespoons kosher salt*

*1 cup rice wine vinegar or white wine vinegar*

*3 tablespoons sugar*

# Spiced Ginger Cake with Candied Ginger Cream

THIS MOIST, LIGHTLY SWEETENED CAKE IS REDOLENT OF FRESH GINGER AND SPICES, MAKING IT IDEAL FOR SERVING FOR BRUNCH OR AS A REFRESHING ALTERNATIVE TO A RICH, HEAVY AFTER-DINNER DESSERT.

*Candied ginger is available at specialty food stores, gourmet food shops, and most candy stores; however, Asian grocery stores usually sell this delicacy for half the price.*

**MAKES 9 TO 12 SERVINGS.** ⌒ **HOT #2**

Preheat oven to 350° F. Generously grease and lightly flour a 10 by-13-inch baking pan.

TO MAKE THE CAKE: In a large bowl, using an electric mixer, beat the sugar and vegetable oil together until pale and smooth, about 3 or 4 minutes. Add the eggs one at a time, beating well after each addition. Add the carrots and ginger and mix well.

Combine the dry ingredients, including the nuts, in a medium bowl; mix well. Add to the egg mixture and mix just until combined. Pour the batter into the prepared pan and bake on the lower rack of the oven for 30 minutes. Rotate to the upper shelf and bake 20 to 25 minutes longer, or until a toothpick inserted into the center of the cake comes out clean. Remove from the oven and cool to room temperature. Run a dull knife around the edges of the cake and cut into serving pieces.

TO MAKE THE CANDIED GINGER CREAM: Place the cream in a medium bowl. Using an electric mixer, beat on high speed until soft peaks form. Add the sugar and liqueur and beat until firm enough to hold its shape but not stiff. Add the finely chopped candied ginger and mix gently.

Spread the top of each piece with some of the Candied Ginger Cream and serve garnished with the sliced candied ginger and mint sprigs.

SPICED GINGER CAKE:

*2 cups granulated sugar*

*1½ cups vegetable oil*

*4 eggs, lightly beaten*

*1½ cups finely grated carrots*

*1½ cups minced peeled fresh ginger root*

*2 cups all-purpose flour*

*2 teaspoons baking powder*

*1½ teaspoons baking soda*

*1 teaspoon salt*

*2½ tablespoons ground ginger powder*

*2½ teaspoons each ground cinnamon and mace*

*1½ cups coarsely chopped toasted walnuts*

CANDIED GINGER CREAM:

*1½ cups heavy cream*

*⅓ cup sifted powdered sugar*

*1 tablespoon ginger liqueur or light rum*

*1 cup finely chopped candied ginger*

*Mint sprigs and thinly sliced candied ginger, for garnish*

# Apple, Ginger, and Mint Sorbet

THIS IS ONE OF MY ALL-TIME FAVORITE FLAVOR COMBINATIONS, SIMULTANEOUSLY FIERY, ICY, AND REFRESHING.
SERVE THIS SORBET AS A PALATE CLEANSER BETWEEN COURSES OR AS AN INVIGORATING DESSERT AFTER A RICH MEAL.
**MAKES 6 TO 8 SERVINGS.** ~ **HOTTER #4**

*3 cups water*

*3 cups sugar*

*5-inch piece fresh ginger root, coarsely chopped*

*1 cup firmly packed, coarsely chopped fresh
    mint leaves*

*2 large tart green apples, peeled, cored, and
    finely chopped*

*⅓ cup fresh lemon juice*

*2-inch piece fresh ginger root, peeled and
    finely chopped*

*20 ice cubes, coarsely crushed*

*Mint sprigs, for garnish*

In a 6-quart heavy-bottomed saucepan, combine the water, sugar, coarsely chopped ginger, and mint. Bring to a boil over high heat, stirring constantly. Boil for 35 to 40 minutes, stirring frequently to prevent the mixture from boiling over, until the mixture is thick and syrupy. Remove from the heat and strain through a fine wire sieve.

Return the syrup to the saucepan and bring to a boil over high heat; cook 3 minutes, stirring constantly. Add the apples and lemon juice and cook 3 to 4 minutes, or until the apples are just tender. Remove from the heat and cool slightly. Add the finely chopped ginger and mix well.

In a blender, puree the mixture until smooth, stopping occasionally to scrape the sides of the container. Transfer to a non-reactive container and freeze for at least 6 hours or up to 2 days. (The mixture won't freeze solid, but it will become slushy.)

Before serving, place half of the ice cubes and half of the fruit mixture in the blender. Blend until the ice is finely crushed and the mixture is smooth and icy. (If you're only serving three or four people, stop at this point and reserve the other half for later.) Blend the remaining ice cubes and fruit mixture. Serve immediately, garnished with sprigs of fresh mint.

# Horseradish

Pan-Fried Potato and Horseradish Cakes

Green Bean Salad with Creamy Almond-Horseradish Dressing

New Potato Salad with Sour Cream–Horseradish Dressing

Smoked Ham and Cabbage Slaw with Horseradish

Roast Beef and Vegetable Rolls with Horseradish Cream Cheese

Smoked Chicken Salad with Horseradish Vinaigrette

Pan-Fried Trout on Spinach with Bacon and Horseradish

Rigatoni with Prawns and Horseradish-Leek Cream

Israeli Horseradish and Beet Condiment

Pork Tenderloin and Cucumber Sandwiches
with Horseradish Mayonnaise

# ORSERADISH

FEW FOODS COME CLOSE TO THE POWER AND INTENSITY OF FRESHLY GRATED HORSERADISH. Once peeled and grated, a fresh root emits a vapor so potent it could penetrate a cement wall.

A member of the *Cruciferae* family, horseradish is a perennial plant native to eastern Europe and western Asia. It now grows in Britain, Russia, northern Europe, and the United States. The plant has long, dark green leaves that can be used in salads and other savory dishes, but it is the root that appears most frequently in prepared foods and condiments.

Approximately the size of a half-dollar in circumference, the ten- to twelve-inch-long root is rough and knobby, with pale yellow to light brown skin tone and ivory-colored, slightly fibrous flesh. Fresh roots must be carefully washed with warm water and a vegetable brush to remove caked-on dirt. Once cleaned, use a sharp paring knife to remove the thin outer skin. At this point you can either grate, finely mince, dice, julienne, or coarsely chop the root.

When buying fresh horseradish, look for hard, relatively unblemished roots that do not yield to bending motions (rubbery roots are past their prime and short on flavor). To store fresh horseradish, loosely wrap in paper towels, place inside a plastic bag, and store in the refrigerator for up to one and a half months. Some people prefer storing the root inside a paper bag, but I feel the additional plastic wrapping provides better insulation. Depending on how fresh the root was when purchased, horseradish can keep for up to three months in the refrigerator. Once opened, prepared commercial horseradish loses potency. Store the condiment in the refrigerator for up to four or five months.

TO GRATE HORSERADISH: As called for in recipes that follow, use the finest setting of the grater.

TO FINELY MINCE HORSERADISH: Slice the root into very thin rounds. Spread the slices on a cutting board, and using a sharp chef's knife or a cleaver, chop into tiny pieces no larger than 1/16 inch.

To COARSELY CHOP HORSERADISH: Follow the same instructions as for finely mincing but chop into rough-sized pieces about ¼ inch in size.

To DICE HORSERADISH: Cut the root into 2- or 3-inch lengths. Depending on the size of the dice (thinner slices for small dice and thicker for large dice), cut the root from top to bottom into long slices. Using three or four slices, make a neat stack. Cut the pieces lengthwise into the desired width, then cut across the thin strips to form the desired-size dice.

To JULIENNE HORSERADISH: Follow the instructions for dicing but omit the last step—simply cut the slices into the desired width, but do not cut across into square dice shapes.

These recipes call for the fresh root in inch lengths, but since roots vary slightly in size, it is impossible to obtain exact measurements for recipes. As with ginger root, precision is not critical. Although I have suggested quantities, adjust the amounts of horseradish called for in recipes to suit your personal taste.

1- TO 2-INCH PIECE FRESH HORSERADISH ROOT = ABOUT ¼ CUP GRATED

2- TO 3-INCH PIECE FRESH HORSERADISH ROOT = ABOUT ½ CUP GRATED

5- TO 6-INCH PIECE FRESH HORSERADISH ROOT = ABOUT 1 CUP GRATED

Fresh horseradish root imparts the greatest essence when grated. It lends a generous amount of flavor when finely minced, and a moderate quantity when diced or coarsely chopped. Like many fresh ingredients, horseradish is most potent in its raw form. Retaining a moderate amount of flavor when heated, fresh horseradish root and prepared horseradish lose most of their intensity when cooked for extended periods of time. For this reason, add the ingredient toward the end of cooking for a pronounced flavor, or after a dish has completely cooled for the most dramatic effect.

The recipes that follow range from mild to scorching; some are saturated with the essence of horseradish while others only hint of it. Strongly infused with the flavor of fresh horseradish are the *New Potato Salad with Sour Cream–Horseradish Dressing* and the *Smoked Ham and Cabbage Slaw with Horseradish*—both are outstanding salads that taste best when served at cool room temperature. *The Roast Beef and Vegetable Rolls with Horseradish Cream Cheese* and the delectable *Pork Tenderloin and Cucumber Sandwiches with Horseradish Mayonnaise* highlight the sinus-clearing qualities of freshly grated horseradish, while the *Green Bean Salad with Creamy Almond-Horseradish Dressing* features the root as a more subtle flavoring agent.

Remember, when preparing fresh horseradish, open the window closest to your work area to allow exit for the pungent fumes. As the recipes in this chapter hopefully will demonstrate, the heady effects and distinctive flavor of fresh horseradish are worth a few tears.

# Pan-Fried Potato and Horseradish Cakes

If you like to start your day with foods more flavorful than cereal or pastry, try these golden brown potato cakes laced with fresh horseradish. For a complete breakfast, pair with eggs and smoked ham or sausages and perhaps a basket of toasted bread.

**Makes 16 cakes; 6 to 8 servings.** ⌇ **Hot #3**

Place the potatoes and 3 quarts of salted water in a large pot. Bring to a boil over high heat. Reduce the heat to moderate and cook about 15 minutes, or until the potatoes are tender but not mushy. Drain well in a colander and place in a large bowl. Using a hand-held potato masher, mash the potatoes to a fine consistency. Set aside until needed.

In a very large sauté pan, cook the onions in the olive oil and butter over high heat for 10 minutes, stirring frequently, until light golden brown. Add the sherry and cook 1 minute. Reduce the heat to moderately low and cook 20 minutes, or until the onions are dark brown, very soft, and sweet. Add the scallions and cook 30 seconds. Add to the potatoes along with the horseradish and sour cream; mix well and season with salt and pepper.

Using about 3 tablespoons per cake, form the potato mixture into 16 discs approximately ½ inch thick. Place the formed cakes in a single layer on sheet pans, cover with plastic wrap or foil, and refrigerate for at least 1½ hours or up to 1 day.

Before cooking coat each cake with the beaten eggs, taking care to completely cover the entire surface of each. Dredge the cakes in the bread crumbs, coating all sides evenly. Return to the refrigerator for 30 minutes, uncovered, or up to 2 hours, covered.

In a very large, nonstick sauté pan, heat about ½ inch of oil over moderately high heat until it is hot, but not smoking. Add some of the cakes, leaving about a ½-inch space between each one.

*4 large baking potatoes, peeled and quartered*

*2 large onions, cut into small dice*

*2 tablespoons olive oil*

*2 tablespoons unsalted butter*

*½ cup dry sherry*

*6 scallions, trimmed and minced*

*6-inch piece fresh horseradish root, peeled and coarsely grated*

*3 tablespoons sour cream, plus additional for drizzling (optional)*

*Salt and pepper, to taste*

*2 eggs, lightly beaten*

*1 cup finely ground bread crumbs*

*¾ to 1 cup vegetable oil, for cooking*

Cook the first side 2 to 3 minutes, or until golden brown. Flip and cook second side until golden brown. Remove using a slotted spatula and place on paper towels to drain. Keep warm in a low oven. Cook the remaining potato cakes, using more oil for cooking as needed. Serve immediately, drizzled with sour cream.

# Green Bean Salad with Creamy Almond-Horseradish Dressing

THE COMBINATION OF TOASTED ALMONDS AND FRESH HORSERADISH MAKES A SURPRISINGLY BALANCED AND
TASTY DRESSING FOR FRESH GREEN BEANS AND SWEET, CRISP RED BELL PEPPER. PAIR WITH COOKED AND COOLED SLICED HAM,
TURKEY, OR PORK LOIN FOR A WARM-WEATHER LUNCH OR SUPPER.

**MAKES ABOUT 6 SERVINGS.** ⌁ HOT #3

CREAMY ALMOND-HORSERADISH DRESSING:

*1 cup walnut or cold-pressed peanut oil*

*⅓ cup white wine vinegar or champagne vinegar*

*4-inch piece fresh horseradish root, peeled and
  coarsely chopped*

*⅔ cup finely chopped toasted almonds*

*2 shallots, halved and thinly sliced*

*½ cup finely chopped fresh parsley*

*2 pounds green beans, trimmed*

*1 medium red bell pepper, stemmed, seeded,
  and cut into slivers*

*Salt and pepper, to taste*

*½ cup coarsely chopped toasted almonds, for garnish*

TO MAKE THE CREAMY ALMOND-HORSERADISH DRESSING: Place the oil, vinegar, horseradish, and finely chopped almonds in a blender. Puree until smooth, stopping occasionally to scrape the sides of the container. Transfer the dressing to a large bowl; add the shallots and parsley and mix well.

Bring 5 quarts of salted water to boil in an 8-quart pot. Have ready a very large bowl filled with ice water. Add the green beans to the boiling water, stir well, and return to the boil. Cook 1 to 2 minutes, or until they are bright green and crisp-tender. Drain immediately in a colander and refresh with cold running water. Immediately plunge the beans into the ice water and swish them around with your hands. When the beans are thoroughly chilled, about 5 minutes, drain in a colander. Dry the green beans in a single layer on kitchen towels or on several layers of paper towels.

Add the green beans to the dressing along with the red bell pepper; toss gently and season with salt and pepper. Serve immediately, garnished with the coarsely chopped almonds.

# New Potato Salad with Sour Cream–Horseradish Dressing

BECAUSE THIS ROBUST POTATO SALAD HAS THE SINUS-CLEARING QUALITIES ASSOCIATED WITH FRESH HORSERADISH, IT HOLDS UP WELL TO GRILLED OR ROASTED MEATS, WILD POULTRY, OR STRONG-TASTING, OILY FISH. WHEN PAIRED WITH SLICED HAM, SMOKED TURKEY, OR ROAST BEEF, IT FORMS A SIMPLE, HOT-WEATHER MEAL. THIS DISH IS BEST MADE ONE DAY AHEAD.

**MAKES ABOUT 6 SERVINGS.** ⌒ **HOTTER #4**

2½ pounds small red new potatoes, quartered

1 small red onion, cut into small dice

2 cups sour cream

⅓ cup apple cider vinegar

4-inch piece fresh horseradish root, peeled and finely grated

½ cup finely chopped fresh parsley

Salt and pepper, to taste

In a 10-gallon pot, bring 6 gallons of salted water to a boil. Add the potatoes and return to the boil. Reduce the heat to moderately high, and cook 12 or 13 minutes, or until tender when pierced with a fork. Drain well in a colander and cool to room temperature. When cool, place in a large bowl.

Combine the red onion, sour cream, vinegar, horseradish, and parsley in a small bowl; mix well. Add to the potatoes and mix gently. Season with salt and pepper and serve immediately, or store in a tightly sealed container in the refrigerator for up to 4 days.

# Smoked Ham and Cabbage Slaw with Horseradish

DELICIOUS ON ITS OWN, YOU MAY ALSO WANT TO TEAM THIS ZESTY COLESLAW WITH
FRIED FISH OR GRILLED CHICKEN FOR A COMPLETE MEAL.
**MAKES ABOUT 6 SERVINGS.** ∼ **HOTTER #4**

Place the cabbage, red onion, and ham in a very large bowl. Place the olive oil in a small bowl. Slowly add the vinegar, whisking constantly with a wire whisk to form a smooth emulsion. Add the prepared horseradish, fresh horseradish, cumin seeds, and sugar; mix well. Add to the cabbage-ham mixture and toss gently. Season with salt and pepper. Serve immediately, or store in a tightly sealed container in the refrigerator for up to 3 days (bearing in mind that the vinegar will cause the cabbage to wilt slightly).

*5 cups white cabbage, finely shredded*

*1 small red onion, halved and thinly sliced*

*¾ pound thinly sliced smoked ham, cut into ¼-inch-wide strips*

*½ cup olive oil*

*¼ cup apple cider vinegar*

*½ cup prepared horseradish*

*5-inch piece fresh horseradish root, peeled and finely grated*

*1½ teaspoons cumin seeds*

*1 teaspoon sugar*

*Salt and pepper, to taste*

# Roast Beef and Vegetable Rolls with Horseradish Cream Cheese

THESE PALATE-TINGLING ROAST BEEF AND VEGETABLE ROLLS MAKE A HANDSOME APPETIZER IDEAL
FOR SERVING AT COCKTAIL PARTIES. THEY ARE SIMPLE TO ASSEMBLE, REQUIRE NO LAST MINUTE PREPARATION,
AND ARE SURE TO PLEASE MEAT- AND VEGETABLE-LOVERS ALIKE.

**MAKES ABOUT 8 SERVINGS. ⌒ HOTTER #5**

TO MAKE THE HORSERADISH CREAM CHEESE: In a medium bowl, combine the cream cheese, horseradish, and lemon zest and mix well.

In a 6-quart pot, bring 4 quarts of salted water to boil over high heat. Have ready a large bowl filled with ice water. Add the green beans and carrots to the boiling water, stir well, and return to the boil. Cook approximately 30 seconds or until both are crisp-tender. Drain well in a colander and refresh with cold running water. Immediately submerge in the ice water, swishing the vegetables around with your hands. When the vegetables are thoroughly chilled, about 5 minutes, drain in a colander. Dry the vegetables in a single layer on kitchen towels or on several layers of paper towels.

Lay the slices of roast beef on a flat surface. Using a wide, dull knife, gently spread about 1½ tablespoons of the cream cheese mixture on each slice. For each roll, make a stack using two green beans, two carrot sticks, and two strips of the bell pepper on top of the cream cheese along the short end of each beef slice. Gently roll the beef around the vegetables, forming a tight cylinder (the tips of the green beans will probably peek out the end of each roll).

Wrap the finished rolls in plastic and refrigerate for at least 1 hour or up to 4 hours. Just before serving, cut each roll in half to expose the cross-section. Serve immediately.

HORSERADISH CREAM CHEESE:

*1 pound natural cream cheese (no gums or stabilizers), softened to room temperature*

*5-inch piece fresh horseradish root, peeled and finely grated*

*Zest from 1 lemon*

*⅓ to ½ pound (about 24) green beans, trimmed*

*2 carrots, cut into 24 sticks approximately 3 inches long and ¼ inch wide*

*Twelve ⅛-inch-thick slices rare roast beef (about 1 pound)*

*1 large yellow bell pepper, stemmed, seeded, and cut into 24 long, thin strips*

# Smoked Chicken Salad with Horseradish Vinaigrette

LESS PUNGENT WHEN FINELY DICED RATHER THAN GRATED, THE HORSERADISH IN THIS DISH ADDS FLAVOR WITH
LESS HEAT, MAKING IT SUITABLE FOR THOSE WITH MORE SENSITIVE PALATES. IF YOU CANNOT FIND WHOLE SMOKED CHICKENS,
FEEL FREE TO USE SMOKED CHICKEN BREAST OR SMOKED TURKEY BREAST CUT INTO CUBES.

**MAKES ABOUT 4 SERVINGS.** ～ **HOT #2**

TO MAKE THE HORSERADISH VINAIGRETTE: Place the peanut oil in a large bowl. Slowly add the vinegar, whisking constantly with a wire whisk to form a smooth emulsion. Add the horseradish and caraway seeds and mix well.

Add the chicken and celery to the vinaigrette, season with salt and pepper, and mix well. Arrange the large butter lettuce leaves around the edge of a large platter and put the small leaves in the center. Mound the salad on top of the small lettuce leaves and garnish with the tomatoes. Serve immediately.

HORSERADISH VINAIGRETTE:

⅔ cup peanut oil

3 tablespoons rice wine vinegar or champagne vinegar

3-inch piece fresh horseradish root, peeled and cut into tiny dice

1 teaspoon caraway seeds

2½ cups shredded smoked chicken meat

2 inner stalks celery, trimmed, thinly sliced on the diagonal, and blanched

Salt and pepper, to taste

6 large butter lettuce leaves, trimmed

6 to 8 small inner butter lettuce leaves, trimmed

4 cherry tomatoes, halved, for garnish

4 yellow pear tomatoes, halved, for garnish

# Pan-Fried Trout on Spinach with Bacon and Horseradish

PAN-FRIED TROUT IS ONE OF MY FAVORITE BREAKFAST DISHES. IN THIS RECIPE, THE DELICATE FLAVOR OF THE FISH IS ACCENTED BY SMOKY BACON, PUNGENT HORSERADISH, AND FRESH SPINACH, RESULTING IN A MEDLEY OF CONTRASTING FLAVORS, TEXTURES, AND COLORS.

*To facilitate chopping the bacon, wrap it tightly in plastic and place in the freezer for twenty minutes prior to cutting.*
**MAKES 4 SERVINGS.** ∽ **HOT #1**

*¾ pound thick-sliced bacon, coarsely chopped*

*4 boneless trout filets (6 to 8 ounces each)*

*All-purpose flour, for dredging*

*2½ tablespoons peanut oil*

*Juice from 1 lemon*

*3-inch piece fresh horseradish root, peeled and minced*

*1 large bunch spinach, stemmed, washed, and dried (about 4 cups packed leaves)*

*Salt and pepper, to taste*

*Lemon wedges, for garnish*

In a large nonstick sauté pan, cook the bacon until brown and crisp. Remove with a slotted spoon and drain on paper towels; set aside. Remove the bacon fat from the pan, reserving 2 tablespoons for cooking and discarding the rest. Wipe the sauté pan clean of any remaining brown bits and return the reserved bacon fat to the pan. Set aside until needed.

Using a clean kitchen towel, pat the trout filets dry on both sides. Dredge the fish in flour, taking care to coat all sides. In a very large sauté pan, heat the peanut oil over moderately high heat until hot, but not smoking. Add the trout, skin sides down, and cook 2 minutes, or until light golden brown. Flip the fish over, add the lemon juice, and reduce the heat to moderate. Cook the second sides 3 to 4 minutes, or until the fish is barely opaque in the center. Remove from the pan, cover with foil, and set aside.

Heat the reserved bacon fat over moderate heat. Add the horseradish, spinach, and reserved bacon and cook, stirring constantly, 30 to 45 seconds, or until the spinach just starts to wilt. Immediately remove from the heat and season with salt and pepper. Arrange the spinach mixture on 1 large platter or divide among 4 individual plates. Place the trout on top of the spinach and serve immediately, garnished with lemon wedges.

# Rigatoni with Prawns and Horseradish-Leek Cream

THE PLEASING SHARP TASTE OF FRESH HORSERADISH COUNTERBALANCES THE RICH QUALITY OF HEAVY CREAM AND FRESH PRAWNS IN THIS SIMPLE-TO-MAKE PASTA DISH. TO ROUND OFF THE MEAL, SERVE WITH A SALAD OF MILD AND BITTER GREENS AND WARM BREAD.

**MAKES ABOUT 6 SERVINGS.** ∽ **HOT #2**

Wash the sliced leeks in a large bowl of cold water, swishing them about with your hands and loosening any dirt or sand from between the layers. Remove the leeks from the water and drain well in a colander. If they are particularly sandy, repeat the procedure a second time, draining thoroughly.

In a very large, shallow saucepan, cook the leeks and garlic in the olive oil over high heat for 5 minutes, stirring frequently, until the leeks are wilted and any moisture has evaporated. Add the cream, tomatoes, horseradish, and thyme and bring to a boil over high heat, stirring constantly to prevent the cream from boiling over. Reduce the heat to moderately high and cook 6 to 8 minutes, stirring frequently, until the cream is thick enough to heavily coat the back of a spoon. Add the prawns and cook 30 seconds, or until they are opaque halfway through. Remove from the heat and set aside until needed.

Bring 6 quarts of salted water to boil in a 9-quart pot. Add the pasta and cook 11 to 12 minutes, or until al dente. Drain well in a colander and place in a very large, preheated bowl.

Heat the sauce over high heat for 30 seconds or just until the prawns are opaque in the center. Take care not to overcook the prawns. Add to the pasta, toss gently, and season with salt and pepper. Garnish with the parsley and serve immediately.

2 leeks, white part only, halved, and thinly sliced

2 cloves garlic, finely chopped

2 tablespoons olive oil

2½ cups heavy cream

2 small tomatoes, cored and cut into small dice

4-inch piece fresh horseradish root, peeled and finely grated

1½ teaspoons dried thyme

½ pound medium prawns, peeled

¾ pound rigatoni pasta

Salt and pepper, to taste

½ cup coarsely chopped fresh parsley

# Israeli Horseradish and Beet Condiment

THIS STUNNING CONDIMENT GOES WELL WITH GRILLED MEATS AND POULTRY, BUT IT TRULY COMPLEMENTS OILY, PUNGENT FISH SUCH AS HERRING, MACKEREL, OR SARDINES. FOR A MORE BITING, SHARPLY FLAVORED MIXTURE WITH A HOMOGENIZED TEXTURE, COARSELY GRATE THE COOKED BEETS AND THE HORSERADISH ROOT INSTEAD OF CUTTING THEM INTO THIN STRIPS.

**MAKES ABOUT 4 CUPS.** ⁓ **HOTTER #6**

*5 medium red beets, trimmed and washed*

*6-inch piece fresh horseradish root, peeled*

*4 cups apple cider vinegar*

*2½ tablespoons each sugar and kosher salt*

Bring 4 quarts of water to boil in a large saucepan. Add the beets and return to the boil. Reduce the heat to moderately high and cook about 15 minutes, or until they yield slightly to the touch but retain a firm interior. Drain in a colander and cool to room temperature. When cool enough to handle, peel the beets and cut into ⅛-inch-thick rounds. Using 3 slices per pile, stack the beet rounds and cut into ⅛-inch-wide strips. Place in a very large bowl and set aside.

Using a very sharp knife, cut the horseradish root crosswise into two 3-inch cylinders. Cut the root lengthwise into ⅛-inch-wide slices. Using three slices per pile, stack the horseradish root and cut into ⅛-inch-wide strips.

Add the horseradish, vinegar, sugar, and salt to the beets and mix gently. Transfer to a glass or stainless steel container with a tight-fitting lid and refrigerate for at least 1 week, preferably 2 weeks, before using. Will keep in the refrigerator for 2 to 3 months.

# Pork Tenderloin and Cucumber Sandwiches
## with Horseradish Mayonnaise

PAIR THIS HEARTY SANDWICH WITH A MUG OF DARK BEER AND THICK-CUT POTATO CHIPS FOR A SATISFYING AUTUMN LUNCH.
THE COMPONENTS FOR THIS RECIPE CAN ALL BE PREPARED ONE DAY IN ADVANCE AND ASSEMBLED JUST BEFORE SERVING.
MAKES 4 SANDWICHES. ∾ HOTTER #6

HORSERADISH MAYONNAISE:

*2 egg yolks, vigorously beaten*

*1 whole egg, vigorously beaten*

*½ cup peanut or vegetable oil*

*¼ cup olive oil*

*2 teaspoons sherry vinegar*

*5-inch piece fresh horseradish root, peeled and finely grated*

*Salt and pepper, to taste*

*Two ⅔- to ¾-pound pork tenderloins, trimmed of fat*

*4 tablespoons prepared horseradish*

*8 thick slices oversized dark bread, such as whole-wheat, nine-grain, or pumpernickel*

*1 English cucumber, peeled and thinly sliced*

TO MAKE THE HORSERADISH MAYONNAISE: Place the egg yolks and whole egg in a medium bowl. Using an electric hand-mixer on low speed, begin adding the peanut oil to the eggs, one drop at a time, beating constantly to form a smooth emulsion. When all the peanut oil has been added, add the olive oil in a very thin stream, beating constantly to maintain a smooth emulsion. Add the vinegar and horseradish and mix well. Season with salt and pepper. Store in a tightly sealed container in the refrigerator until ready to use.

Preheat oven to 450° F.

Coat the pork tenderloins on all sides with the prepared horseradish. Place the tenderloins on a flat, greased roasting rack set over a lightly greased baking dish. Roast for 10 to 12 minutes, or until the center is just barely pink. Take care not to overcook the pork. Remove from the oven and cool to room temperature. When cool, cut into thin slices. (If time allows, wrap the cooked and cooled tenderloins in plastic or foil and refrigerate for 1 day. Thoroughly chilled meat is much easier to cut into thin slices, and the meat keeps well.)

Evenly distribute the Horseradish Mayonnaise among the bread slices, spreading an even layer on each. Arrange 5 or 6 rounds of cucumber on 4 of the bread slices and top with the sliced pork. Cover each with a second slice of bread and press gently to secure the filling. Cut in half and serve immediately.

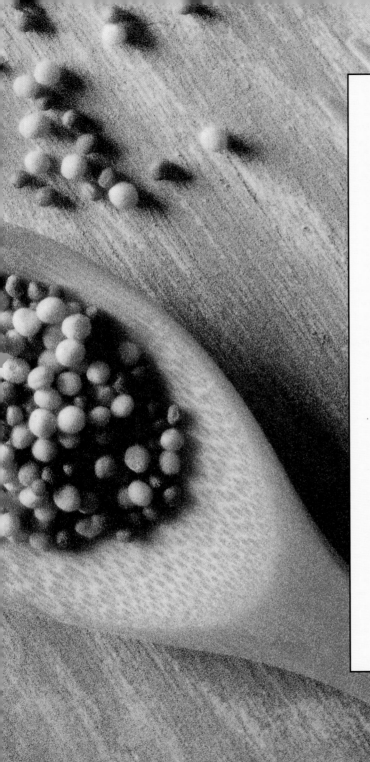

# Mustard

Chinese-Style Mouth-Fire Dipping Sauce

Creamy Mustard, Potato, and Leek Gratin

Caramelized Onion-Mustard Tart with Gruyère Cheese

Ham and Rice Salad with Two Mustards

Melted Cheddar and Sweet Pickle Sandwiches
with Two Mustards

Sweet and Spicy Bell Pepper–Mustard Relish

Mustard- and Honey-Braised Brussels Sprouts

Baked Macaroni with Mustard and Cheddar Cheese

Irene's Mustard-Glazed Ham Loaf

Grilled Chicken Wings with Two Mustards and Honey

# ℳustard

Through the centuries mustard has been used for medicinal as well as culinary purposes. Ancient Greeks used the seeds for their curative properties and for flavoring foods, or, more accurately, for disguising the taste of rancid meats. It was the Romans, however, who combined the seeds with vinegars, honey, spices, and nuts to form the first prepared mustard pastes. The name is thought to come from the Roman mixture of crushed mustard seeds and *must* (unfermented grape juice), which was called *mustum ardens,* or "burning wine."

A member of the *Cruciferae* family, mustard plants are annuals which produce bright yellow flowers and long, narrow, seed-filled pods. Black mustard, native to the Middle East and Asia, has been cultivated in Europe for centuries. Because this particular seed is difficult to harvest, it has not been widely cultivated for mass production. Brown mustard seed, originally from Asia, now grows throughout northern Europe and in parts of England. Less pungent than its black counterpart, this seed is favored by many mustard makers, who use it to produce full-flavored, pungent pastes. Native to the Mediterranean, yellow mustard seeds are now grown in eastern counties of England, and in Canada and the United States. Less pungent than the black or brown seeds and larger than both, yellow seeds are used primarily in English, French, some German, and many American mustards; they are also ground and sold as mustard powder.

When purchasing whole mustard seeds, look for regular, even-colored, hard seeds. Store them in a tightly sealed jar or plastic bag in a cool, dark place for up to one year. Purchase mustard powder in individual sealed tins rather than in bulk, where it tends to lose its strength and intensity. Prepared commercial mustards must be refrigerated once opened; properly stored, mustards are good for four or five months, but those kept longer tend to lose their potency and flavor.

When mustard seeds are crushed and mixed with cold or warm water, the enzyme myrosin mixes with the glucoside contained in the seeds and forms a volatile oil that is a desirable characteristic of mustard. However, myrosin mixed with boiling water produces a bitter, unpleasant flavor, rendering the finished product undesirable. For this reason, use cold water when making homemade mustards. Like horseradish, fresh ginger, and many chili peppers, prepared mustard loses most of its punch when cooked for extended periods of time. For the most pronounced flavor, add slightly crushed seeds or mustard paste at the end of cooking rather than at the beginning. Whole mustards seeds can be added at any time during the cooking process. Prepared mustards act as a natural thickener, and since mustard is so low in calories and fat, it is a sensible and delicious thickening agent for many dishes.

Commercial mustards range from mild and smooth to sharp, biting, and coarse in texture. When cooking, intensely hot, pungent mustards naturally lend more flavor to cooked or heated dishes than do those with less emphatic properties. Although most mustards are exhilarating to the taste buds, there is a wide spectrum of heat intensity. Likewise, depending on the type of mustard used and the way it is used in a dish, some of the following recipes are tame and understated while others pack a punch. For example, the *Chinese-Style Mouth-Fire Dipping Sauce* is tremendously hot and fiery while the *Caramelized Onion–Mustard Tart with Gruyère Cheese* is mellow and subtle.

The flavor of mustard can take center stage, but it also can work nicely in a supporting cast of flavors, lending nuances to dishes without overwhelming them. Mustard plays a dominant role in dishes such as *Grilled Chicken Wings with Two Mustards and Honey* and *Sweet and Spicy Bell Pepper–Mustard Relish,* but it serves more as a background flavor in *Creamy Mustard-Potato-Leek Gratin* and *Baked Macaroni with Mustard and Cheddar Cheese.*

When blended with other ingredients, mustard takes the role of a flavoring agent rather than one that supplies fire. Still, these tiny little seeds and prepared pastes lend a penetrating, distinctive, and welcome accent to a delectable variety of foods and dishes.

# Chinese-Style Mouth-Fire Dipping Sauce

PRESENT THIS INTENSELY FLAVORED MUSTARD-BASED DIPPING SAUCE TO THOSE WHO ADORE THE HEAD-TINGLING
QUALITIES OF MUSTARD POWDER COMBINED WITH RAW GARLIC AND FIERY CHILI PASTE. "ORIENTAL-STYLE" DRY MUSTARD
PACKED IN TINS IS AVAILABLE IN ASIAN MARKETS, SPECIALTY FOOD SHOPS, AND MOST GROCERY STORES.

**MAKES ABOUT 1 CUP. ~ HOTTEST #9**

½ cup "Oriental-Style" dry mustard

¾ cup cold water

2 tablespoons soy sauce

1 tablespoon sesame oil

1 tablespoon sherry vinegar

1 to 2 teaspoons Asian-style red chili paste

2 cloves garlic, finely minced

Salt and pepper, to taste

Place the dry mustard in a small bowl. Slowly add the water, whisking constantly with a wire whisk to form a smooth emulsion. Add the soy sauce, sesame oil, vinegar, chili paste, garlic, salt, and pepper; mix well. Let stand at room temperature for at least 1 hour before serving, although it's best to store the sauce in a tightly sealed container in the refrigerator for several days before using. Will keep for up to 3 months in the refrigerator, but it is best if used within 1 month.

# Creamy Mustard, Potato, and Leek Gratin

COLEMAN'S MUSTARD POWDER AND WHOLE YELLOW MUSTARD SEEDS ADD DEPTH AND TEXTURE TO THIS CLASSIC POTATO DISH.
RICH, CREAMY, AND ROBUST IN FLAVOR, THE GRATIN PAIRS WELL WITH GRILLED STEAKS OR LAMB, OR WITH ROASTED CHICKEN.
FOR A SATISFYING VEGETARIAN MEAL, SERVE THE WARM GRATIN ON A BED OF MIXED BABY GREENS AND ACCOMPANY WITH HOT ROLLS.

**MAKES ABOUT 8 SERVINGS.** ⁓ **HOT #1**

Preheat oven to 375° F. Lightly grease a 9-by-12-inch baking pan.

In a large sauté pan, cook the leeks, garlic, and mustard seeds in the butter over moderately high heat for 5 minutes, stirring frequently. Set aside.

Arrange one third of the potatoes in a single layer on the bottom of the baking pan; evenly distribute one half of the leek mixture over the top. Arrange half of the remaining potatoes over the leeks, making an even layer. Cover with the remaining leeks. Make the final layer using the remaining potatoes.

Place the Coleman's mustard in a medium bowl. Slowly add the cream a little at a time, whisking with a wire whisk to form a smooth mixture. Season with salt and pepper. Slowly pour the mustard cream over the potatoes. Bake on the middle rack of the oven for 1½ hours, or until the potatoes are very tender and the sauce is very thick. Remove from the oven and let stand at room temperature for 7 to 10 minutes before cutting into squares. Serve immediately.

2 large leeks, trimmed (white part only) halved, and thinly sliced

2 cloves garlic, finely chopped

1½ tablespoons yellow mustard seeds

3 tablespoons unsalted butter

6 large baking potatoes, peeled, halved, and cut into ¼-inch-thick slices

⅓ cup Coleman's dry mustard

2 cups heavy cream

Salt and pepper, to taste

# Caramelized Onion–Mustard Tart with Gruyère Cheese

LONG, SLOW COOKING YIELDS SWEET, MILD-FLAVORED ONIONS THAT COMBINE BEAUTIFULLY WITH THE NUTTY TASTE OF GRUYÈRE CHEESE, SWEET TOMATOES, AND PUNGENT DRY MUSTARD IN THIS SAVORY TART.

**MAKES 6 TO 8 SERVINGS.** ∼ **HOT #2**

TO MAKE THE TART SHELL: Place the flour, mustard seeds, and salt in a medium bowl and mix well. Using your fingers, mix in the butter, rubbing it against the flour until the mixture resembles coarse meal. Still mixing with your fingers, add just enough ice water to form the mixture into a ball. Flatten into a disc and wrap tightly in plastic. Refrigerate for at least 2 hours or up to 2 days. Remove from the refrigerator 30 minutes before rolling.

Preheat oven to 350° F. Lightly grease a 12-inch tart pan with a removable bottom.

On a lightly floured surface, roll the dough into a circle approximately 14 inches in diameter. Gently fit the dough into the pan, making the edge extend about ¼ inch above the sides of the pan to allow for shrinkage while baking. Cover the bottom and sides of the dough with parchment paper or foil and fill with pie weights or dried beans. Bake for 15 minutes. Remove the pie weights and bake an additional 10 minutes, or until the bottom and sides are light golden brown. Remove from the oven and cool to room temperature. Increase oven temperature to 450° F.

TO MAKE THE FILLING: In a very large sauté pan, cook the onions in the olive oil over high heat for 10 minutes, stirring frequently. Add the garlic, sherry, and thyme and cook 1 minute. Reduce the heat to moderately low and cook 30 to 35 minutes, stirring frequently, until the onions are very soft, golden brown, and sweet. Remove from the heat and transfer to a bowl. When cool, add the Coleman's mustard and cheese and mix well. Season with salt and pepper. Arrange the filling in the tart shell, making an even layer all the way to the edges. Evenly cover with the tomato slices.

Bake on the top shelf of the oven for 12 or 13 minutes, or until the filling is hot and the tomatoes are wilted. Remove from the oven and cool slightly before cutting into wedges to serve.

TART SHELL:

1¾ cups all-purpose flour

1 tablespoon yellow mustard seeds

2 teaspoons kosher or sea salt

6 tablespoons unsalted butter, cut into very small pieces

4 to 5 tablespoons ice water

FILLING:

4 very large onions, quartered and cut into ¼-inch-wide wedges

3 tablespoons olive oil

3 cloves garlic, finely chopped

½ cup dry sherry

1 teaspoon dried thyme

¼ cup Coleman's dry mustard

½ pound imported Gruyère cheese, finely grated

Salt and pepper, to taste

2 small tomatoes, cut into ⅛-inch-thick slices

# Ham and Rice Salad with Two Mustards

THIS COLORFUL SALAD IS SIMPLE TO PREPARE AND TRAVELS WELL,
MAKING IT AN IDEAL SUMMER BARBECUE OR PICNIC DISH.
**MAKES ABOUT 6 SERVINGS.** ⌁ **HOT #2**

¼ cup olive oil

¼ cup peanut or vegetable oil

3 tablespoons red wine vinegar

3 tablespoons white wine mustard or
   champagne mustard

1 tablespoon honey

2 cloves garlic, minced

½ teaspoon each ground coriander, fennel seeds,
   and cumin

1½ cups long-grain brown rice

Two ¼-inch-thick slices smoked ham
   (about ⅔ pound), finely chopped

1 red bell pepper, stemmed, seeded, and cut into
   small dice

1½ cups finely chopped mustard greens

Salt and pepper, to taste

Large mustard green leaves, for lining platter

Place the olive and peanut oils in a small bowl. Slowly add the vinegar, whisking constantly with a wire whisk to form a smooth emulsion. Add the mustard, honey, garlic, and spices and whisk until thoroughly incorporated. Set the dressing aside.

Bring 3 quarts of water to boil over high heat in an 8-quart pot. Add the rice, stir well, and return to a boil. Reduce the heat to moderately high and cook 35 to 40 minutes, or until the rice is al dente. Drain well in fine-sieved colander and place in a large bowl. Cool slightly.

Add the ham, bell pepper, and dressing to the rice; toss well. When the mixture is completely cool, add the mustard greens and mix well. Season with salt and pepper. Serve slightly chilled or at room temperature on a platter lined with the mustard green leaves.

# Melted Cheddar and Sweet Pickle Sandwiches with Two Mustards

A LUNCH COMPOSED ON THIS PIQUANT SANDWICH, A GREEN SALAD, THICK-CUT POTATO CHIPS,
AND A GLASS OF DARK BEER IS SURE TO BRIGHTEN ANY RAINY DAY.

**MAKES 4 SERVINGS.** ～ **HOT #2**

¼ cup Dijon mustard

¼ cup coarse-grained English or German mustard

⅓ cup finely chopped sweet pickles

4 thick slices dense whole-wheat, light rye,
  or multi-grain bread

½ pound sharp English or Canadian cheddar
  cheese, cut into 16 slices

8 thin tomato slices

Preheat broiler portion of oven.

In a small bowl, combine the mustards and pickles and mix well. Arrange the bread slices on a baking sheet small enough to fit under the broiler. Spread each slice of bread with one fourth of the mustard-pickle mixture and top with the cheese slices, dividing equally. Make sure the cheese is fairly level and the slices extend to the edges of the bread.

Broil in the oven until the cheese is melted and bubbly. Remove from the broiler, top each with tomato slices, and return to the broiler for 1 minute, or until the tomatoes are slightly wilted and warmed through. Serve immediately.

# Sweet and Spicy Bell Pepper—Mustard Relish

This assertive-tasting, colorful relish depends on honey mustard for a mild, sweet tone, Coleman's dry mustard for a sharp edge, and coarse-grained mustard for body and texture. Excellent paired with sausages of all varieties, this relish also can be used as an accompaniment to roasted chicken, pork, beef, or lamb, or as a condiment when making sandwiches.

**Makes 4 to 6 servings.** ∼ **Hot #2**

In a very large, nonstick sauté pan, cook the onion, coriander, and caraway seeds in the olive oil over high heat for 2 to 3 minutes, stirring frequently. Add the bell peppers and cook 4 to 5 minutes, stirring frequently, until they are just wilted. Remove from the heat and place in a large bowl; cool to room temperature.

In a small bowl, combine the honey and coarse-grained mustards, the dry mustard, and the vinegar; mix well. Add to the vegetables and mix gently. Season with salt and pepper. Transfer to a nonreactive container, cover tightly, and refrigerate for at least 1 day before serving. Will keep in the refrigerator for up to 7 days.

*1 medium yellow onion, halved and thinly sliced*

*2 teaspoons ground coriander*

*½ teaspoon caraway seeds*

*2 tablespoons olive oil*

*1 large red bell pepper, stemmed, seeded, and thinly sliced*

*1 large green bell pepper, stemmed, seeded, and thinly sliced*

*1 large yellow or gold bell pepper, stemmed, seeded, and thinly sliced*

*¼ cup honey mustard*

*¼ cup coarse-grained mustard*

*1½ tablespoons Coleman's dry mustard*

*1½ tablespoons white wine vinegar*

*Salt and pepper, to taste*

# Mustard- and Honey-Braised Brussels Sprouts

EVEN THOSE USUALLY DISINTERESTED IN BRUSSELS SPROUTS MAY BE TEMPTED BY THESE MUSTARD- AND HONEY-GLAZED VEGETABLES. THIS AUTUMNAL SIDE DISH COMPLEMENTS ROASTED POULTRY AND FRESH PORK OR HAM.

**MAKES ABOUT 6 SERVINGS. ⌁ HOT #1**

⅓ cup Dijon mustard

1½ tablespoons honey

3 shallots, halved and thinly sliced

2 cloves garlic, finely chopped

2 tablespoons unsalted butter

1 tablespoon olive oil

½ cup dry sherry

1½ pounds Brussels sprouts, trimmed and halved

1 cup homemade chicken stock or low-sodium chicken broth

Salt and pepper, to taste

In a small bowl, combine the mustard and honey. Set aside.

In a large sauté pan, cook the shallots and garlic in the butter and oil over moderate heat for 3 minutes, stirring frequently. Add the sherry and cook 5 minutes, or until it has almost evaporated.

Add the Brussels sprouts and chicken broth to the sauté pan and bring to a boil over high heat. Reduce the heat to moderate, cover with a tight-fitting lid, and cook 13 to 15 minutes, or until the sprouts are tender. Remove the lid, add the mustard-honey mixture and cook 1 to 2 minutes over high heat, stirring frequently, until the sauce coats the vegetables and is heated through. Season with salt and pepper and serve immediately.

# Baked Macaroni with Mustard and Cheddar Cheese

A HEALTHY DOSE OF DIJON MUSTARD AND WHOLE YELLOW MUSTARD SEEDS ADDS AN ADDITIONAL LAYER
OF FLAVOR AND TEXTURE TO THIS AMERICAN CLASSIC. WHILE TERRIFIC AS A MAIN DISH,
IT ALSO GOES WELL WITH BAKED HAM OR PORK CHOPS OR WITH ROASTED OR SMOKED POULTRY.
**MAKES 6 TO 8 SERVINGS.** ～ **HOT #2**

¾ pound elbow macaroni pasta

2 tablespoons unsalted butter

¼ cup all-purpose flour

1½ tablespoons yellow mustard seeds

1 teaspoon ground cumin

2 cups half-and-half, warmed

½ cup whole milk, warmed

¾ pound sharp yellow cheddar cheese, coarsely grated

⅓ cup Dijon mustard

Salt and pepper, to taste

Preheat oven to 400° F. Generously grease a round, deep-sided, 4-quart baking dish.

In a 10-quart pot, bring 7 quarts of salted water to boil over high heat. Add the macaroni, stir vigorously, and return to a boil. Cook 7 minutes, stirring occasionally, until almost al dente. Drain well in a colander and place in a large bowl. Cover with a damp kitchen towel or place a piece of plastic wrap directly on top of the pasta. Set aside.

In 3-quart, heavy-bottomed saucepan, melt the butter over moderately low heat. Add the flour, mustard seeds, and cumin and mix well. Cook 7 or 8 minutes, stirring frequently, until the mixture is very pale brown and smells nutty.

Slowly add about ¾ cup of the half-and-half, whisking constantly with a wire whisk to prevent lumps from forming and to make a smooth emulsion. Slowly add the remaining half-and-half, whisking constantly to avoid forming lumps. When all the cream has been added, add the milk and mix well, scraping the bottom of the pan with a wooden spoon. Bring to a boil over high heat and cook 2 minutes, whisking constantly. Reduce the heat to moderate and cook 10 to 12 minutes, stirring frequently to prevent the bottom from scorching. Remove from the heat. (If the sauce has any lumps, press the mixture through a fine wire sieve into a large bowl; return the strained mixture to the saucepan.) Add three fourths of the cheese to the hot cream mixture and stir until thoroughly melted. Add the mustard and mix well.

Add the cream mixture to the macaroni and toss gently. Season with salt and pepper and turn into the prepared baking dish. Bake on the bottom shelf of the oven for 20 minutes, or until the center is piping hot. Evenly distribute the remaining cheese over the top and return to the top shelf of the oven. Bake 5 minutes longer, or until the cheese is melted and starting to bubble. Remove from the oven and serve immediately.

# Irene's Mustard-Glazed Ham Loaf

VARYING SLIGHTLY FROM MY MOM'S HAM LOAF, THIS RENDITION CALLS FOR BOTH DRY MUSTARD AND WHOLE MUSTARD SEEDS. TO MAKE A COMPLETE MEAL, PAIR THIS SATISFYING MEAT LOAF WITH A GREEN SALAD OR BRAISED CABBAGE, AND SWEET POTATOES OR LENTILS. PASS AN ASSORTMENT OF MUSTARDS TO SATISFY THOSE WHO SIMPLY CAN'T GET ENOUGH OF THE STUFF.

*If freshly ground pork and smoked ham are not readily available in your market, you can grind the meat yourself using a food processor or meat grinder.*

**MAKES 6 TO 8 SERVINGS. ～ HOT #2**

*3 tablespoons light brown sugar*

*3 tablespoons Coleman's dry mustard*

*3 tablespoons apple cider vinegar*

*1 pound finely ground boneless smoked ham*

*1 pound finely ground fresh lean pork shoulder*

*1 cup finely ground Ritz crackers*

*3 tablespoons whole yellow mustard seeds*

*1 teaspoon black pepper*

*2 eggs, lightly beaten*

*¾ cup whole milk*

Preheat oven to 350° F. Lightly grease an 8½-by-4½-inch loaf pan.

To make the glaze, in a small bowl combine the brown sugar, dry mustard, and vinegar to form a smooth mixture. Set aside.

In a large bowl, place the ham, pork, crackers, mustard seeds, pepper, eggs, and milk. Using your fingers, gently mix the ingredients until just combined. Do not overmix. Transfer the mixture to the prepared loaf pan and smooth the top. Using a sharp fork, poke holes into the entire surface of the ham loaf. Bake on the lower shelf of the oven for 35 minutes.

Remove the ham loaf from the oven and carefully pour the glaze over the top, making sure it goes into the meat rather than over the sides of the pan! Return to the oven and bake on the top shelf 10 to 12 minutes, or until the glaze is hot and several shades darker. Let stand at room temperature for 10 minutes before cutting into 1-inch-thick slices. Serve immediately.

# Grilled Chicken Wings with Two Mustards and Honey

STICKY, GOOEY, AND IRRESISTIBLE, THESE SLIGHTLY SWEET-SAVORY HOT CHICKEN WINGS MAKE
A SENSATIONAL OPENING FOR ANY SUMMER MEAL.

**MAKES ABOUT 6 SERVINGS.** ∼ **HOT #2**

½ cup prepared Chinese-style mustard

½ cup Dijon mustard

½ cup honey

2 tablespoons teriyaki sauce

4 cloves garlic, minced

1 teaspoon black pepper

3½ pounds meaty chicken wings

In a bowl large enough to accommodate all the wings, combine the mustards, honey, teriyaki sauce, garlic, and black pepper; mix well, forming a smooth paste. Add the chicken wings and toss well to evenly coat the wings. Cover with foil or plastic and refrigerate for 6 hours or up to 1 day.

Prepare a charcoal grill. When the coals are medium-hot (covered with a thin layer of white ash), place the wings on the grill. Cook, rotating the wings as they brown and brushing them occasionally with the marinade, for 15 to 17 minutes (depending on the heat of the barbecue), or until the exteriors are dark golden brown and crispy and the interiors are cooked through. Remove from the grill and serve immediately.

# PEPPERCORNS

Scallop-Corn Chowder with Pink and White Peppercorns

Broccoli and Red Bell Pepper Salad with
Black and White Peppercorns

Chinese Hot and Sour Soup

Peppery Chicken-Fried Rice

Pasta with Peppered Artichokes, Ham, and Toasted Almonds

Mediterranean Seafood Stew with Fennel and Peppercorns

Poached Chicken Breasts with Peppercorn Sauce

Seared Four-Peppercorn Swordfish with Coriander

Vanilla Rice Pudding with Green and Pink Peppercorns

Chocolate-Hazelnut Mousse with Black Pepper

# EPPERCORNS

PEPPER, THE WORLD'S MOST POPULAR SPICE, WAS AT ONE TIME SO UNCOMMON IT WAS CONSIDERED as precious as gold, and in some instances it was used as currency. Nowadays pepper is plentiful and inexpensive; still a valuable spice to the home cook, it is nevertheless taken for granted and unfortunately rarely plays a dominant role.

Native to Indonesia and the tropical forest and equatorial regions of India, pepper is still cultivated in Indonesia and India as well as Malaysia, Brazil, the West Indies, eastern Asia, Cambodia, and Madagascar. *Piper nigrum,* a species of *Piper,* is a climbing plant with 3- to 7-inch heart-shaped green leaves and flowers that bear clustered fruit. Depending on their level of maturity and how they are treated once picked, these fruits eventually come to market as either black, white, or green peppercorns.

BLACK PEPPERCORNS, picked before they fully ripen, are dried in the sun for eight to ten days until they shrink and shrivel and are hard, dry, and black. There are many varieties of black pepper, each with a distinctive taste and aroma. Most popular are Tellicherry and Lampong peppercorns, but well-stocked specialty or spice shops often carry Singapore, Penang, and Alleppey varieties as well.

Traditionally used solely for savory dishes, slightly crushed or whole black peppercorns are beginning to appear in baked goods and other confections. I particularly like pairing dark chocolate with the spice, but it also marries well with such dried fruits as prunes, figs, and dates, as well as such fresh fruits as melon, berries, plums, pears, and figs.

WHITE PEPPERCORNS are picked ripe and then treated to a water bath to remove the outer skins. Once the skin is rubbed off, the inner portion is dried until it turns a pale shade of off-white. In comparison to the black peppercorn, the white variety is smaller and softer, contains a higher percentage of piperine (a heat-lending alkaloid), but fewer aromatic elements, thus rendering it more fiery but less flavorful. The most common types available include Muntok, Sarawak, and Siam.

White peppercorns are good to use when you want a more direct, pointed, and fiery effect rather than one with complex and multilayered characteristics. Although they are normally used in savory dishes, white peppercorns also lend a warm, aromatic, almost fruity flavor to select desserts.

GREEN PEPPERCORNS are picked unripe, but unlike those processed to make black peppercorns, they are immediately freeze-dried or preserved in brine. Less pungent than black or white peppercorns, fruity-tasting green peppercorns are traditionally paired with milder tasting meats, such as chicken, pork and veal, and with fish and seafood. While traveling in Thailand, I sampled several dishes that included small bunches of fresh green peppercorns on the stem—they were extremely pungent!

PINK PEPPERCORNS, technically speaking, are not considered true pepper but rather the dried berries from a South American tree. According to some references, this under-utilized spice is derived from *Shinus terebinthifolius;* others list the source as *Shinus molle.* In any event, pink peppercorns are usually freeze-dried or packed in brine and can be found in specialty food stores or spice shops. Use these aromatic, slightly sweet, distinctive, and pungent peppercorns in cream or butter sauces; with poultry, fish, and seafood; and in desserts that beg for a flowery, spicy flavor followed by a hint of warmth.

When purchasing dried peppercorns, look for whole peppercorns sold in bulk or packed in tightly sealed tubes or containers. To check the freshness, rub a few peppercorns between your fingers and sniff for a pronounced aroma. Black and white pepper are sold preground, but avoid purchasing pepper in this form. Preground pepper often includes fillers and other unwanted ingredients and is usually stale.

I recommend grinding dry peppercorns in a spice or coffee mill for cooking purposes. For the table I prefer an adjustable pepper mill so that the peppercorns can be ground fine, medium, or coarse. A mortar and pestle is convenient for extremely coarse grinding and bruising.

To BRUISE PEPPERCORNS in a mortar and pestle, place the spice in the center of the mortar and lightly rub with the pestle until the desired texture is achieved. To bruise or grind without a pepper mill, mortar and pestle, or electric grinder, place the spice in a medium-sized bowl and use a smaller bowl that will fit inside it to rub and crush the peppercorns. You can also place the peppercorns on a cutting board and press gently with a heavy skillet or rolling pin until they are bruised. If you try to bruise or crush the peppercorns too aggressively at first they will fly all over the room. Be gentle until they are bruised and then, if desired, you can use more force to grind them smaller.

The recipes in this chapter are undoubtedly among the most unique in this collection. Unlike ginger, mustard, horseradish, and chili peppers, peppercorns are relatively underused and underappreciated, even by seasoned cooks. Classic dishes that highlight this spice are few in number, so I therefore developed recipes that showcase the four distinctly different peppercorns especially for this book.

My favorites in this chapter include *Broccoli and Red Bell Pepper Salad with Black and White Peppercorns; Pasta with Peppered Artichokes, Ham, and Toasted Almonds;* and *Seared Four-Peppercorn Swordfish with Coriander,* all of which contain a moderate amount of heat provided by at least two different peppercorns. More penetrating and fiery are *Peppery Chicken-Fried Rice* and *Poached Chicken Breasts with Peppercorn Sauce.*

In addition to the savory recipes, I have included two unique desserts: *Vanilla Rice Pudding with Green and Pink Peppercorns,* which takes on an almost floral quality from the pepper, and the dusky, intensely flavored *Chocolate-Hazelnut Mousse with Black Pepper,* which generates a warm, spicy effect on the palate.

Whether included in savory or sweet dishes, I hope these recipes will highlight the culinary versatility of this neglected spice.

# Scallop-Corn Chowder with Pink and White Peppercorns

FINELY GROUND WHITE PEPPERCORNS ADD HEAT AND WHOLE PINK PEPPERCORNS LEND A WARM, FLORAL NOTE TO THIS RICH CHOWDER. TEAM WITH A GREEN SALAD AND WARM DINNER ROLLS FOR A LIGHT SUPPER.

**MAKES ABOUT 8 SERVINGS.** ~ **HOT #2**

In a 10-quart, heavy-bottomed saucepan, cook the onion in the peanut oil and butter over moderately high heat for 7 minutes, stirring frequently. Add the white peppercorns, coriander, fennel seeds, and wine and bring to a boil over high heat. Cook, stirring frequently, 3 to 4 minutes, or until the wine is almost evaporated. Add the clam juice, cream, and pink peppercorns and cook 15 minutes, stirring frequently, until the mixture is the consistency of heavy cream.

Add the corn and cook 3 minutes. Add the scallops and cook 1½ to 2 minutes, stirring frequently, or until the scallops are just opaque in the center. Take care not to overcook the scallops. Season with salt and black pepper, if desired. Serve immediately, garnished with the chives.

*1 large onion, cut into small dice*

*2 tablespoons peanut or vegetable oil*

*1 tablespoon unsalted butter*

*2 tablespoons coarsely ground white peppercorns*

*½ tablespoon ground coriander*

*1 teaspoon ground fennel seeds*

*¾ cup dry white wine*

*5 cups clam juice*

*2½ cups heavy cream*

*1 tablespoon whole pink peppercorns*

*2 large ears corn, shaved (about 2 cups fresh corn kernels)*

*1 pound scallops, small side muscles removed*

*Salt and black pepper, to taste*

*½ cup finely chopped fresh chives, for garnish*

# Broccoli and Red Bell Pepper Salad with Black and White Peppercorns

SERVE THIS COLORFUL, ROOM TEMPERATURE SALAD AS A SIDE DISH OR ACCOMPANIED
WITH BREAD STICKS FOR A LIGHT, HEALTHFUL LUNCH.

*When exposed to vinegar (or other acids) for more than twenty or thirty minutes, green vegetables take on an unpleasant gray tone, losing their crunchy texture and vivid color. For this reason, if you plan to hold this salad longer than twenty minutes before serving, either omit the vinegar when making the vinaigrette and sprinkle the dressed vegetables with the vinegar just before serving, or prepare the vegetables and the vinaigrette separately and combine the two just before serving.*

MAKES ABOUT 6 SERVINGS. ⌒ HOTTER #4

In an 8-quart saucepan, bring 4 quarts of salted water to boil over high heat. Have ready a large bowl filled with ice water. Drop the broccoli into the boiling water and stir well. Cook 30 to 45 seconds or until the broccoli is crisp-tender and bright green. Drain in a colander and refresh with cold water. Immediately plunge into the ice water and swish around using your hands. When the broccoli is thoroughly chilled, drain well in a colander. Lay the broccoli in a single layer on clean kitchen towels and pat dry. Place in a large bowl along with the red bell pepper.

In a small bowl, combine the olive oil and peppercorns. Slowly add the vinegar, whisking constantly with a wire whisk to form a smooth emulsion. Add the garlic and salt and mix well. Add to the vegetables and toss gently. Adjust the seasoning and sprinkle with pine nuts. Serve immediately.

*8 cups broccoli florets (about 2 large heads)*

*1 large red bell pepper, stemmed, seeded, and julienned*

*½ cup olive oil*

*1½ teaspoons each finely ground white and black peppercorns*

*1 tablespoon each slightly crushed white and black peppercorns*

*2 tablespoons balsamic vinegar*

*2 cloves garlic, minced*

*Salt, to taste*

*½ cup toasted pine nuts*

# Chinese Hot and Sour Soup

PEPPERY, SOUR, AND SLIGHTLY SWEET FLAVORS FORM THE BACKBONE OF THIS CLASSIC CHINESE SOUP.
YOU MAY INCREASE THE AMOUNT OF PEPPERCORNS IF YOU CRAVE EXTRA HEAT.

*To facilitate slicing the pork, wrap the meat tightly in plastic and place in the freezer for thirty minutes prior to cutting.
You can buy all of the ingredients in any Asian market and some well-stocked grocery or natural food stores.*
MAKES 8 TO 10 SERVINGS. ⁓ HOTTEST #7

¾ cup rice wine vinegar

2½ tablespoons cornstarch

8 dried Chinese black mushrooms

3 dried cloud ear mushrooms

10 cups homemade chicken stock or low-sodium chicken broth

3 tablespoons each finely ground white and black peppercorns

3 tablespoons soy sauce

1½ teaspoons Chinese-style hot chili paste

1½ tablespoons peanut oil

½ pound pork tenderloin, cut into slivers approximately 2 inches long and ⅛ inch wide

4 cloves garlic, minced

1⅓ cups julienned bamboo shoots

Two 5-ounce blocks firm tofu, cut into ¼-inch cubes

3 eggs, lightly beaten

Salt and additional black pepper, to taste

5 scallions, trimmed and cut on the diagonal into ½-inch pieces

In a small bowl, combine the vinegar and cornstarch; mix well. Set aside.

Soak the black and cloud ear mushrooms in warm water to cover for 10 to 15 minutes, or until soft and pliable. Drain well and discard the soaking liquid. Remove the stems and discard. Coarsely chop the black mushrooms, and cut the cloud ear mushrooms into long slivers approximately ⅛ inch wide. Place in a 6-quart, heavy-bottomed saucepan.

To the mushrooms add the chicken stock, ground pepper, soy sauce, and chili paste. Bring to a boil over high heat and cook 7 minutes, stirring occasionally. Reduce the heat to moderately low while you prepare the remaining ingredients.

In a large, nonstick sauté pan, heat the peanut oil over high heat until it just begins to smoke. Add the pork, garlic, and bamboo shoots and cook 30 seconds, stirring constantly. Add to the stock along with the vinegar-cornstarch mixture and tofu, and bring to a boil over high heat. Cook, stirring frequently, for 3 to 4 minutes, or until the soup is thick and aromatic.

Slowly add the eggs in a thin stream, stirring gently with a large fork to make long, delicate strands. Remove from the heat and season with salt and more pepper, if desired. Add the scallions just before serving.

# Peppery Chicken-Fried Rice

A LIVELY MIXTURE OF COARSELY GROUND AND WHOLE PEPPERCORNS GIVES THIS CLASSIC CHINESE DISH A DEFINITE KICK.
TO FACILITATE CUTTING THE CHICKEN INTO SMALL PIECES, WRAP THE BONED AND SKINNED BREASTS IN PLASTIC AND FREEZE FOR
THIRTY MINUTES PRIOR TO DICING. YOU MAY SUBSTITUTE DICED SMOKED HAM FOR THE CHICKEN IF YOU WISH.

**MAKES ABOUT 6 SERVINGS.** ⟳ **HOTTEST #7**

Bring 4 quarts of salted water to boil in an 8-quart pot. Add the rice, stir well, and return to a boil. Cook 10 minutes, or until the rice is just tender. Take care not to overcook the rice. Drain in a colander and refresh with cold water. Spread the rice in a thin layer on a baking sheet and refrigerate until cold. Alternatively, cover with plastic or foil and refrigerate overnight.

In a very large nonstick sauté pan or wok, heat the oil over high heat until it just begins to smoke. Add the chicken, bell pepper, ginger, scallions, garlic, and peppercorns and cook 1 minute, stirring constantly. Add the green peas, cooked rice, soy sauce, and vinegar and cook 1 minute, stirring constantly.

Make a large well in the center of the rice mixture, clearing a space in the pan. Add the eggs and cook, stirring frequently, until they just begin to set—like scrambled eggs. Immediately remove the pan from the heat. Using a fork, stir the eggs into the rice mixture. Serve immediately with additional soy sauce on the side, if desired.

*1½ cups long-grain white rice*

*¼ cup peanut oil*

*2 boneless, skinless chicken breast halves, cut into ¼-inch cubes*

*1 red or yellow bell pepper, stemmed, seeded, and cut into small dice*

*2-inch piece fresh ginger root, peeled and finely chopped*

*6 scallions, trimmed and finely chopped*

*3 cloves garlic, finely chopped*

*1 tablespoon each coarsely ground black and white peppercorns*

*2 teaspoons each whole pink and green peppercorns*

*1 cup cooked English green peas*

*2½ tablespoons light soy sauce*

*1½ tablespoons rice wine vinegar*

*6 eggs, well beaten*

# Pasta with Peppered Artichokes, Ham, and Toasted Almonds

THIS PASTA DISH COMBINES SOME OF MY FAVORITE INGREDIENTS. I PREFER USING FRESH BABY ARTICHOKES, BUT IF YOU ARE PRESSED FOR TIME, OR IF YOU CANNOT FIND THE FRESH VERSION, SUBSTITUTE PRECOOKED, MARINATED ARTICHOKE HEARTS SOLD IN JARS. STRAIN THE CHOKES BEFORE USING THEM IN THE PASTA, BUT SAVE THE MARINATING LIQUID TO USE IN OTHER DISHES.

**MAKES 6 TO 8 SERVINGS.** ～ **HOT #3**

1 large onion, cut into medium dice

4 cloves garlic, finely chopped

⅔ cup olive oil

1 tablespoon finely ground white peppercorns

2 teaspoons drained whole green peppercorns packed in brine

1 teaspoon dried thyme

1 cup dry white wine

1½ cups cooked baby artichoke hearts, quartered

Two ½-inch slices smoked ham (about 1 pound), cut into ½-inch cubes

1 pound medium-sized pasta shells

⅓ pound imported Parmesan cheese, finely grated

½ cup coarsely chopped toasted almonds

Salt and black pepper, to taste

In a very large, nonstick sauté pan, cook the onion and garlic in 3 tablespoons of the olive oil over moderately high heat for 7 minutes, stirring frequently. Add the peppercorns, thyme, and wine and cook 5 minutes, stirring occasionally. Add the artichoke hearts and ham and mix gently. Remove from the heat and set aside until needed.

In a 10-quart pot, bring 7 quarts of salted water to a boil over high heat. Add the pasta and stir well. Return to a boil and cook 12 to 13 minutes, or until the pasta is al dente. Drain well in a colander and immediately place in a very large bowl. Add the remaining olive oil and toss well.

Reheat the vegetable-ham mixture over high heat, stirring constantly, just until heated through, about 1½ minutes. Add to the pasta along with half of the grated cheese and the almonds. Season with salt and pepper and toss gently. Serve immediately, and pass the remaining cheese on the side.

# Mediterranean Seafood Stew with Fennel and Peppercorns

DON'T BE INTIMIDATED BY THE LONG LIST OF INGREDIENTS, MANY OF WHICH ARE HERBS AND PEPPERCORNS THAT REQUIRE NO PREPARATION. THIS ZIPPY SEAFOOD STEW TAKES LESS THAN ONE HOUR TO MAKE, AND WHEN COUPLED WITH HOT BREAD AND A SALAD, MAKES A WONDERFULLY INVITING DISH FOR COMPANY.

*When buying the fresh mussels and clams, be sure to purchase only those with closed shells.*

**MAKES 6 TO 8 SERVINGS. ～ HOTTER #6**

4 cloves garlic, thinly sliced

2 large bulbs fennel, trimmed, halved, cored, and cut into ½-inch dice

1 tablespoon drained whole green peppercorns packed in brine

1 tablespoon coarsely ground black peppercorns

2 teaspoons each slightly crushed white and pink peppercorns

¼ cup olive oil

½ teaspoon each dried rosemary, thyme, and oregano

3 medium tomatoes, cored and finely diced

1 cup dry white wine

1½ pounds fresh mussels (about 20 to 22), beards removed and shells scrubbed

1 pound Manila or any other small fresh clams (about 18 to 20), shells scrubbed

4 cups clam juice or strong fish stock

8 small new potatoes, cut into eighths

¾ pound medium prawns, peeled and tails removed

¾ pound scallops, small side muscles removed

Salt and additional black pepper, to taste

½ cup finely chopped fresh parsley, for garnish

In a large, heavy-bottomed saucepan, cook the garlic, fennel, and peppercorns in the olive oil over moderate heat for 7 to 8 minutes, stirring frequently. Add the herbs, tomatoes, and wine and bring to a boil over high heat; cook 3 minutes, stirring frequently. Add the mussels and clams, cover with a tight-fitting lid, and cook 3 or 4 minutes, stirring once or twice. Remove the lid and, using kitchen tongs, remove all mussels and clams with opened shells; place in a bowl and set aside. Return the lid to the pot and cook an additional minute; remove all mussels and clams with opened shells and add to the others. Discard any with closed shells.

Add the clam juice and potatoes to the pot. Return to the boil and cook 12 to 15 minutes, or until the potatoes are tender. Meanwhile, remove the mussels and clams from their shells, place in a small bowl, and set aside. Discard the shells.

Add the prawns and scallops to the stew and cook 1½ minutes, stirring frequently. Add the reserved mussels and clams and cook 30 seconds, or just until the prawns and scallops are cooked through and the shellfish is hot. Take care not to overcook the seafood. Season with salt and more pepper, if desired. Serve immediately, garnished with the parsley.

# Poached Chicken Breasts with Peppercorn Sauce

COOL IN TEMPERATURE YET WARM IN FLAVOR, THIS ELEGANT CHICKEN DISH GOES WELL WITH A GREEN SALAD,
FRESH CORN, OR STEAMED ASPARAGUS FOR A PLEASING HOT-WEATHER SUPPER.

**MAKES 4 SERVINGS.** ~ **HOTTER #5**

In a shallow saucepan, place the chicken, wine, water, and peppercorns. (The chicken should be completely submerged in liquid, so add additional water and/or wine to cover, if necessary.) Bring to a boil over high heat. Reduce the heat to moderately low, cover tightly, and simmer 10 to 12 minutes, or until the chicken is just cooked through. Remove the chicken with a slotted spoon, reserving the liquid, and drain in a colander. Cool chicken to room temperature. When cool, keeping the breast meat intact, remove and discard the skin, bones, cartilage, and tendons. Cover the chicken breasts with a damp kitchen towel and set aside.

To make the sauce, cook the reserved poaching liquid over high heat, stirring frequently, for 30 to 35 minutes, or until reduced to about ⅓ cup. Transfer to a medium bowl and cool to room temperature. When cool, add the mayonnaise and season with salt and more pepper, if desired. Serve the chicken breasts slightly chilled or at room temperature, topped with the sauce and garnished with the parsley.

*4 large chicken breast halves*

*3 cups dry white wine*

*3 cups water*

*1½ teaspoons coarsely ground black peppercorns*

*1½ teaspoons whole pink peppercorns*

*1 teaspoon drained whole green peppercorns
    packed in brine*

*½ cup mayonnaise, preferably homemade*

*Salt and additional black pepper, to taste*

*Sprigs of parsley, for garnish*

# Seared Four-Peppercorn Swordfish with Coriander

ASK YOUR FISHMONGER TO SLICE EXTRA-THICK STEAKS FROM THE WHOLE FISH WHEN PURCHASING THE
SWORDFISH FOR THIS RECIPE. SERVED HOT OR CHILLED, THESE PEPPERCORN- AND CORIANDER-ENCRUSTED STEAKS ARE
TERRIFIC SERVED WITH HOMEMADE AIOLI OR SIMPLY DRIZZLED WITH FRESH LEMON JUICE.

**MAKES 4 SERVINGS.** ∽ **HOTTER #5**

In a small bowl, combine the peppercorns, salt, coriander, and 3 tablespoons of the olive oil; mix well. Pat the mixture on both sides of each swordfish steak, slightly pressing the peppercorns and coriander into the fish. Let stand at room temperature for 15 minutes.

In a large, nonstick sauté pan, heat the remaining 2 tablespoons olive oil over moderately high heat. When the oil is hot but not smoking, add the fish steaks and cook 2 minutes on the first side. Gently flip the steaks over and cook second side 2 to 3 minutes, or until the steaks are cooked on the exterior but still pink in the center. Remove the fish from the pan and transfer to a large platter or individual plates. Serve immediately, garnished with lemon wedges.

*2 tablespoons each coarsely ground black and white peppercorns*

*1 tablespoon each coarsely ground pink and green peppercorns*

*1 tablespoon kosher or sea salt*

*2 rounded teaspoons ground coriander*

*5 tablespoons olive oil*

*Four 1-inch-thick swordfish steaks (about 8 ounces each), patted dry*

*Lemon wedges, for garnish*

# Vanilla Rice Pudding with Green and Pink Peppercorns

HEADY WITH THE ESSENCE OF VANILLA, EACH BITE OF THIS DESSERT DELIVERS A SURPRISE PUNCH PROVIDED BY
PINK AND GREEN PEPPERCORNS. PRESENTED WARM IN THE COOLER MONTHS OR CHILLED DURING SUMMERTIME,
THIS UNIQUE RICE PUDDING IS SURE TO STIMULATE TASTE BUDS ANY TIME OF YEAR!

**MAKES 6 TO 8 SERVINGS.** ⌒ HOT #3

4 cups half-and-half

1 teaspoon finely ground pink peppercorns

½ teaspoon each whole pink and green peppercorns

½ teaspoon finely ground black peppercorns

1 vanilla pod, split lengthwise and beans removed

¾ cup short-grained white rice, such as arborio

¾ cup sugar

Pinch salt

½ teaspoon each ground cinnamon and nutmeg

2 cups whole milk

Juice from 1 large orange

Zest from 1 lemon

2 teaspoons vanilla extract

In a 6-quart saucepan, place the half-and-half, peppercorns, and vanilla beans. Bring to a boil over high heat, stirring constantly to prevent the liquid from boiling over. Reduce the heat to moderate and simmer, stirring frequently, for 10 minutes.

Add the rice, sugar, salt, cinnamon, and nutmeg and bring to a boil over high heat. Reduce the heat to moderate and cook 15 minutes, stirring frequently. Add the milk and cook about 40 minutes, stirring occasionally, until the rice is very tender and the mixture is thick and creamy.

Add the orange juice, lemon zest, and vanilla extract; mix well and cook 2 minutes. Remove from the heat. Serve immediately or cool to room temperature, transfer to a storage container, and cover the surface with plastic wrap. Refrigerate until thoroughly chilled.

# Chocolate-Hazelnut Mousse with Black Pepper

MEDIUM-GROUND BLACK PEPPERCORNS LEND A DEEP, WARM ACCENT TO THIS RICH, HAZELNUT-SCENTED CHOCOLATE MOUSSE.
SERVE WITH FRANGELICO OR ESPRESSO FOR A MEMORABLE DESSERT.

*If you cannot find superfine sugar (super-granulated white sugar) in the grocery store, make your own by placing regular granulated sugar in a food processor or blender and processing until fine, five to seven minutes. Do not overprocess the sugar or it will turn to powder.*

**MAKES ABOUT 6 SERVINGS. ~ HOT #2**

*10 ounces high-quality bittersweet chocolate, coarsely chopped*

*2 cups heavy cream*

*3 tablespoons superfine sugar*

*2 tablespoons Frangelico liqueur (or any hazelnut-flavored liqueur)*

*1 tablespoon medium-ground black peppercorns*

*2 extra-large egg whites*

*½ cup finely chopped toasted hazelnuts, for garnish*

In the top of a double boiler set over simmering water, combine the chocolate, ½ cup of the heavy cream, and the sugar, Frangelico, and black pepper. Cook for 2 to 3 minutes, stirring constantly, until the chocolate is completely melted and the mixture is smooth. Remove from the heat and cool to room temperature.

In a small, chilled bowl, whip the remaining 1½ cups heavy cream until stiff peaks form. Refrigerate until needed.

In a small bowl, whip the egg whites until soft peaks form. Gently fold the egg whites into the cooled chocolate mixture until just combined. Gently fold in the whipped cream until thoroughly blended. Do not overmix or the mousse will have an unpleasant texture. Cover with plastic or foil and refrigerate for at least 4 hours, or up to 2 days. Remove the mousse from the refrigerator 30 minutes before serving. Stir well and spoon into attractive glasses or small bowls and garnish with the hazelnuts.

## Index of Recipes

## E

**ENTRÉES**

Caramelized Onion-Mustard Tart
   with Gruyère Cheese, 81
Chinese Stir-Fried Beef with Ginger, 43
Irene's Mustard-Glazed Ham Loaf, 90
Melted Cheddar and Sweet Pickle
   Sandwiches with Two Mustards, 84
Pan-Fried Potato and Horseradish Cakes, 59
Pan-Fried Trout on Spinach with
   Bacon and Horseradish, 68
Poached Chicken Breasts with
   Peppercorn Sauce, 107
Pork Tenderloin and Cucumber Sandwiches
   with Horseradish Mayonnaise, 73
Seared Four-Peppercorn Swordfish
   with Coriander, 109
Ethiopian Onion- and Ginger-Stuffed Jalapeños, 23

## G

Ginger Chicken Salad with Cashew Nuts, 40
Gingered Chicken Liver Spread with Currants, 39
Gingered Spring Vegetable and Salmon Soup, 46
Green Bean Salad with Creamy Almond-
   Horseradish Dressing, 60
Grilled Chicken Wings with
   Two Mustards and Honey, 92

## H

Ham and Rice Salad with Two Mustards, 82

## I

Irene's Mustard-Glazed Ham Loaf, 90
Israeli Horseradish and Beet Condiment, 70

## M

Mediterranean Seafood Stew with
   Fennel and Peppercorns, 106
Melted Cheddar and Sweet Pickle
   Sandwiches with Two Mustards, 84
Mustard- and Honey-Braised Brussels Sprouts, 86

## N

New Potato Salad with Sour Cream–
   Horseradish Dressing, 62

## P

Pan-Fried Potato and Horseradish Cakes, 59
Pan-Fried Trout on Spinach with Bacon
   and Horseradish, 68
Pants-on-Fire Black Bean Soup, 25
**PASTA**
   Baked Macaroni with Mustard and
      Cheddar Cheese, 89
   Cold Noodles with Asian Vegetables
      and Ginger Peanut Sauce, 45
   Pasta with Peppered Artichokes, Ham,
      and Toasted Almonds, 104
   Rigatoni with Prawns and
      Horseradish-Leek Cream, 69
Peppery Chicken-Fried Rice, 103
Pickled Ginger, 49

# Table of Equivalents

The exact equivalents in the following tables have been rounded for convenience.

## US/UK

OZ=OUNCE     LB=POUND

TBL=TABLESPOON     FL OZ=FLUID OUNCE

QT=QUART

## Metric

G=GRAM

KG=KILOGRAM

MM=MILLIMETER

CM=CENTIMETER

ML=MILLILITER

L=LITER

## Weights

| US/UK | Metric |
|---|---|
| 1 OZ | 30 G |
| 2 OZ | 60 G |
| 3 OZ | 90 G |
| 4 OZ (1/4 LB) | 125 G |
| 5 OZ (1/3 LB) | 155 G |
| 6 OZ | 185 G |
| 7 OZ | 220 G |
| 8 OZ (1/2 LB) | 250 G |
| 10 OZ | 315 G |
| 12 OZ (3/4 LB) | 375 G |
| 14 OZ | 440 G |
| 16 OZ (1 LB) | 500 G |
| 1 1/2 LB | 750 G |
| 2 LB | 1 KG |

## Oven Temperatures

| Fahrenheit | Celsius | Gas |
|---|---|---|
| 250° | 120° | 1/2 |
| 275° | 140° | 1 |
| 300° | 150° | 2 |
| 325° | 160° | 3 |
| 350° | 180° | 4 |
| 375° | 190° | 5 |
| 400° | 200° | 6 |
| 425° | 220° | 7 |
| 450° | 230° | 8 |
| 475° | 240° | 9 |
| 500° | 260° | 10 |

## Liquids

| US | Metric | UK |
|---|---|---|
| 2 TBL | 30 ML | 1 FL OZ |
| 1/4 CUP | 60 ML | 2 FL OZ |
| 1/3 CUP | 80 ML | 3 FL OZ |
| 1/2 CUP | 125 ML | 4 FL OZ |
| 2/3 CUP | 160 ML | 5 FL OZ |
| 3/4 CUP | 180 ML | 6 FL OZ |
| 1 CUP | 250 ML | 8 FL OZ |
| 1 1/2 CUPS | 375 ML | 12 FL OZ |
| 2 CUPS | 500 ML | 16 FL OZ |
| 4 CUPS/1 QT | 1 L | 32 FL OZ |

# Equivalents for Commonly Used Ingredients

## All-Purpose (Plain) Flour/
## Dried Bread Crumbs/Chopped Nuts

| | | |
|---|---|---|
| ¼ CUP | 1 OZ | 30 G |
| ⅓ CUP | 1 ½ OZ | 45 G |
| ½ CUP | 2 OZ | 60 G |
| ¾ CUP | 3 OZ | 90 G |
| 1 CUP | 4 OZ | 125 G |
| 1 ½ CUPS | 6 OZ | 185 G |
| 2 CUPS | 8 OZ | 250 G |

## Whole-Wheat (Wholemeal) Flour

| | | |
|---|---|---|
| 3 TBL | 1 OZ | 30 G |
| ½ CUP | 2 OZ | 60 G |
| ⅔ CUP | 3 OZ | 90 G |
| 1 CUP | 4 OZ | 125 G |
| 1 ¼ CUPS | 5 OZ | 155 G |
| 1 ⅔ CUPS | 7 OZ | 210 G |
| 1 ¾ CUPS | 8 OZ | 250 G |

## Brown Sugar

| | | |
|---|---|---|
| ¼ CUP | 1 ½ OZ | 45 G |
| ½ CUP | 3 OZ | 90 G |
| ¾ CUP | 4 OZ | 125 G |
| 1 CUP | 5 ½ OZ | 170 G |
| 1 ½ CUPS | 8 OZ | 250 G |
| 2 CUPS | 10 OZ | 315 G |

## White Sugar

| | | |
|---|---|---|
| ¼ CUP | 2 OZ | 60 G |
| ⅓ CUP | 3 OZ | 90 G |
| ½ CUP | 4 OZ | 125 G |
| ¾ CUP | 6 OZ | 185 G |
| 1 CUP | 8 OZ | 250 G |
| 1 ½ CUPS | 12 OZ | 375 G |
| 2 CUPS | 1 LB | 500 G |

## Long-Grain Rice/Cornmeal

| | | |
|---|---|---|
| ⅓ CUP | 2 OZ | 60 G |
| ½ CUP | 2 ½ OZ | 75 G |
| ¾ CUP | 4 OZ | 125 G |
| 1 CUP | 5 OZ | 155 G |
| 1 ½ CUPS | 8 OZ | 250 G |

## Dried Beans

| | | |
|---|---|---|
| ¼ CUP | 1 ½ OZ | 45 G |
| ⅓ CUP | 2 OZ | 60 G |
| ½ CUP | 3 OZ | 90 G |
| ¾ CUP | 5 OZ | 155 G |
| 1 CUP | 6 OZ | 185 G |
| 1 ¼ CUPS | 8 OZ | 250 G |
| 1 ½ CUPS | 12 OZ | 375 G |

## Grated Parmesan/Romano Cheese

| | | |
|---|---|---|
| ¼ CUP | 1 OZ | 30 G |
| ½ CUP | 2 OZ | 60 G |
| ¾ CUP | 3 OZ | 90 G |
| 1 CUP | 4 OZ | 125 G |
| 1 ⅓ CUPS | 5 OZ | 155 G |
| 2 CUPS | 7 OZ | 220 G |